KNOWING THE FUTURE

MAKING LIFE COUNT
New Life SERIES

PAUL L. WALKER

PATHWAY PRESS
Cleveland, Tennessee

Library of Congress Catalog Card Number 76-710
I.S.B.N. 0-87148-477-3

Prepared and produced by Pathway Press,
Cleveland, Tennessee 37311
© Copyright MCMLXXVI by Pathway Press,
Cleveland, Tennessee 37311

KNOWING THE FUTURE

Larry L. Benz, Editorial Research

Joan Almand, Contributor

Joy Wooderson, Contributor

James Padgett, Cover

Johnny Potter, Design

CONTENTS

A teaching kit for individual or group study with this book is available from Pathway Press.

CONTEMPORARY CLUES

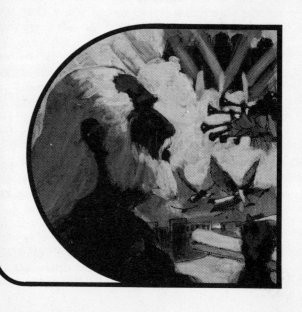

On February 9, 1971, a sudden thrusting movement within the broad network of the San Andreas
fault cost sixty-four lives near Los Angeles. Yet, in
spite of this devastating earthquake, just two and
one-half months later business was going on as usual. Millions continued to ignore this warning, and
today Californians are living all along this 600-
mile fracture in the earth's crust just as though there
will never be another earthquake.

But the Bible tells us differently. As we read
Matthew 24 and 25 we learn from Jesus Christ
Himself that far more than severe earthquakes are
in store for us. Indeed, these will be just the beginning of many sorrows as God's judgment is
poured out upon His people in recompense for centuries of disobedience and lawlessness.

We pick up the narrative in Matthew 24:1 as
Jesus was leaving the Temple. His disciples were
admiring the beautiful stones of the building and
the intricate designs in the architecture, and Jesus
said to them: "You see all these? . . . I tell you
every stone will be thrown down till there is not a
single one left standing upon another" (Matthew
24:2; *Phillips*). Later, as He was sitting on the
slope of the Mount of Olives, His disciples came to

7

Him privately and said, "Tell us, when will this happen? What will be the signal for your coming and the end of this world?" (Matthew 24:3; *Phillips*).

Of all the questions asked of Jesus by His disciples, these were probably the most important. The pages of our daily newspapers tell of starvation in Biafra, crises in the Middle East, and earthquakes in Central America. Men everywhere are seeking answers to serious questions about the future. There has been an overwhelming revival of interest in the occult. Astrology, fortune-telling, Ouija boards, seances, and the like are enjoying an all-time high in popularity.

But we, as Christians, turn to the Word of God for our answers and, in seeking to know what lies ahead, find that He has given us the key to a future He has planned for us that is beyond our wildest imaginings. We find God in the book of Revelation bringing to a conclusion the story of His creation, which was begun in Genesis. In Genesis, we see, Satan became the god of this earth and the prince of power of the air. But in the book of Revelation, we read that Satan will be defeated. He will be bound for a thousand years and ultimately destroyed. In the book of Genesis, we see, the gates of Paradise were shut. But in the book of Revelation, we read that the gates will be opened and man will be fully admitted into the kingdom of God.

In Genesis pain began; in Revelation there will be no more pain. In Genesis night began; in Revelation there will be no more night. In Genesis tears began; in Revelation there will be no more

8

tears. In Genesis sorrow began; in Revelation there will be no more sorrow. In Genesis man was exiled; in Revelation he will inherit all things. (Read Genesis 3:1-24 and Revelation 20:1-10; 21:1-7.)

Thus, as we return to the discussion between Christ and His disciples in Matthew 24, we find that there are certain signs we can look for:

1. False christs (v. 5)
2. Wars and rumours of wars (v. 6)
3. Famines and pestilences (v. 7)
4. Persecution (v. 9)
5. Betrayal (v. 10)
6. False prophets (v. 11)
7. Abounding iniquity (v. 12)
8. World evangelization (v. 14)
9. The abomination of desolation (v. 15)
10. Great tribulation when all God's wrath will be let loose (v. 21)

The signs of Christ's coming are in the process of being fulfilled. In addition to earthquakes and famines, worldwide depression and inflation, violence of all kinds rampant in our cities and brought into our living rooms via television, we find the words of the Apostle Paul in 2 Timothy 3:1-5 to be alarmingly characteristic of the world in which we live:

> But understand this, that in the last days there will set in perilous times of great stress and trouble—hard to deal with and hard to bear.
>
> For people will be lovers of self and [utterly] self-centered, lovers of money and aroused by an inordinate (greedy) desire for wealth, proud and arrogant and contemptuous boasters. They will be abusive (blasphemous, scoffers), disobedient to parents, un-

9

grateful, unholy and *profane.*

[*They will be*] *without natural (human) affection (callous and inhuman), relentless—admitting of no truce* or *appeasement.* [*They will be*] *slanderers—false accusers, trouble makers; intemperate* and *loose in morals* and *conduct, uncontrolled* and *fierce, haters of good.*

[*They will be*] *treacherous (betrayers), rash* [*and*] *inflated with self-conceit.* [*They will be*] *lovers of sensual pleasures* and *vain amusements more than* and *rather than lovers of God.*

For [*although*] *they hold a form of piety (true religion), they deny* and *reject* and *are strangers to the power of it—their conduct belies the genuineness of their profession (Amplified).*

Well, what about it? Just how close are we to the end of this age? In some respects we might say that wars, famines, pestilences, and the like have been with us for generations. Are there any clues to lead us to believe more specifically that we are the generation of which Christ spoke?

Actually there are three major events that must take place before Christ returns. Let us examine them in the light of the technological trends of our times.

1. The Temple must be rebuilt in Jerusalem.

The Bible tells us that five Temples will be built in Jerusalem during its history:

1. Solomon's Temple
2. The Temple restored by Zerubbabel
3. Herod's Temple (Built at the close of the Old Testament era, this Temple is the one in which Jesus preached. It was destroyed in A.D. 70.)
4. The Tribulation Temple (Daniel 7; 9; Matthew 24:15; 2 Thessalonians 2:4; Revelation 11)

5. The Millennial Temple (Ezekiel 40:1-48)

Since Israel was declared a nation in 1948 by the United Nations, the world has been watching with keen anticipation to see when the fourth Temple will be built. In 1974, a newspaper article written by George W. Cornell, religious editor for the Associated Press in New York, read like this:

An aura of mystery surrounds the idea of restoring the Jewish temple in Jerusalem. To many Christians and Jews it is a longed-for dream—a Messianic sign. It is not yet, but something like it is happening. Construction is due to begin in the next few days on the first large central Jewish house of worship in the Holy City since the destruction of the temple 1,904 years ago.

"No one is suggesting that this means the restoration of the temple," says Rabbi Dr. Maurice A. Jaffe, president of the Union of Israel Synagogues which is sponsoring the project. But there are parallels. For one thing the prospective new Jerusalem Great Synagogue is planned as a central representative sanctuary to which Jewish pilgrims from all over the world may come to pray just as they did to the temple of old. In another aspect, every Jew everywhere is being encouraged to contribute something to the building of the new edifice even if only a half shekel which is the basic tribute of each practicing Jew to the ancient temple. Furthermore, the new house of worship is being built of a special radiant stone like that of the temple of Bible times and is to be situated next to the headquarters of Israel's Rabbinic authority, as was the historic temple.

There are many analogies, but we are wary of drawing comparisons. Dr. Jaffe said in an interview, "One gets in hot water even to hint at such a thing. Conditions are out of the question for reestablishing the temple." But what does that sound

11

like to you? For years the Zionist Movement has been gathering money toward the Temple, and it has been rumored that the stones for the Temple edifice are already cut and can be shipped into Jerusalem at any time and at a moment's notice.

2. The entire world must be evangelized.

The second thing that must occur before we can begin to consider the imminence of Christ's second coming is that the whole world must be evangelized. Jesus said, "This good news of the kingdom will be proclaimed to men all over the world as a witness to all the nations, and then the end will come" (Matthew 24:14; *Phillips*).

At this point this has not happened. Over one thousand tribes have never heard the name of Jesus. Many nations have never been touched by the gospel. But plans are underway by Campus Crusade for Christ, Evangelism International, and missionary endeavors of many denominations to use the vast new communications media, Telstar, and others for world evangelization; and it is estimated that within the next ten years every country on the face of the globe will have heard the gospel preached and the name of Jesus Christ will have been proclaimed to all as Savior and Lord.

3. A worldwide community must be established.

The scene may not be exactly right for the appearance of the Antichrist. However, it seems that the mark of the beast and the kind of economy that could result in the frightening events portrayed in the thirteenth chapter of the book of Revelation could take place almost anytime. But consider this:

the July 5, 1974, edition of *The Kiplinger Washington Letter* stated: "Some of the things we are seeing today are the result of our involvement in the worldwide economy . . . what happens in other parts of the world has a direct effect on us." The *Wall Street Journal* of May, 1973, finds the United States open to a "world monetary system that might include gold as a part of it but not necessarily a major part."

We look for a day when computers will control the monetary systems of the world. The technology is less than ten years away. Here's how it will work: Every person will be assigned a number. It will be a three-row, six-digit number and will be stamped on the forehead or in the right hand of each person. In order to buy or sell the person will walk through a scanner, which will pick up the number and transmit it to the bank, which will debit or credit his account as necessary. No money will exchange hands. It won't be needed. This is being considered as the answer to the world's monetary problems.

Remember? Three rows, six digits in each number? Have you read Revelation 13 lately? Speaking of the beast out of the earth, it says:

> Then it compels all, small and great, rich and poor, free men and slaves, to receive a mark on their right hands or on their foreheads. The purpose of this is that no one should be able to buy or sell unless he bears the mark of the name of the animal or the number of its name. Understanding is needed here: let every thinking man calculate the number of the animal. It is the number of a man, and its number is six hundred and sixty-six (Revelation 13: 16-18; *Phillips*).

Right now we know that on microfilm every single individual's life history—economical, spiritual, educational, political, marital, and otherwise —can be put into a kind of filing system so that it can be called up within seconds. It appears that if this were to come to pass, it could be the means of a single person or group of persons literally controlling the reins of the whole world.

We have seen that the stage is set. There are enough clues to convince even the most hardened skeptic. It sounds like the beginning of a horrible nightmare doesn't it?

Let us turn back to the book of Revelation, which brings to a conclusion the story of God's creation, which was begun in Genesis. As we consider this book, certain things stand out.

First, we realize that God is in control of history. He will have the last word. Next, we see that the future can be predicted with some degree of accuracy. In order to understand and to see clearly the overall picture of God's plan for our future, we must begin with the nation of Israel—God's chosen people, who must assume the responsibility for the rejection of the Messiah.

As we attempt to see this plan in view of contemporary times, we find that the Scriptures prophesied in no less than seven places that the nation of Israel would be regathered and restored to the land of Palestine. The history of the Jewish people became a history of a race constantly struggling to survive in the alien countries to which they were scattered. For 2,500 years the Jewish people lived in exile without self-government. They existed in almost every nation of the world and became in

14

many ways an integral part of the culture of those nations; yet, they miraculously retained their own national identity. They endured one captivity after another throughout their development and experienced some of the most appalling sufferings ever forced by one human being upon another.

At the end of World War II the growing Zionist party began working underground in a secret movement to transport the wandering survivors to their "Promised Land." Eventually when the state of Israel came into existence on May 15, 1948, the total Jewish population was 655,000. Most of these people had arrived in a destitute condition and had to be provided with shoes, clothing, housing, employment, education, and medical care. Also, some way had to be found for them to be integrated into the new state.

Today the population of Israel numbers approximately four million. Israel's struggles to hold on to the little piece of land that is her own are not over. Nonetheless, the wanderers have returned to their native land! Who, but God, could have inspired writers to make a prediction 2,500 years ago that defies history and human nature and yet is fulfilled before our very eyes? The answer can only lie in a God who keeps His promises to His covenant people. He is a God who is faithful.

We know that the nation of Israel is the focal point for God's judgment and that the central thrust of God's dealings with the people of the earth will be to bring Israel to full repentance and to punish the nations that have persecuted them. The final chapter will be written in the Middle East, but the repercussions of God's judgment will be felt in every part of the globe.

2

THE
UNFOLDING
DRAMA

Bible Reading:
Revelation 1:4, 9-11
2:2-28; 3:1-21

Imagine yourself banished to a lonely island, bound in chains, poorly fed and clothed, and made to sleep on the bare ground. This was the life John the Apostle faced as a prisoner of the Romans because of his witness for Christ.

And yet in the midst of this persecution, God used John as an even greater witness to reveal to His church the things that were to come . . .

> John, To the seven churches in the province of Asia: . . .
> I, John, your brother and companion in the suffering and kingdom and patient endurance that are ours in Jesus, was on the island of Patmos because of the word of God and the testimony of Jesus. On the Lord's Day I was in the Spirit, and I heard behind me a loud voice like a trumpet, which said: "Write on a scroll what you see and send it to the seven churches: to Ephesus, Smyrna, Pergamos, Thyatira, Sardis, Philadelphia and Laodicea" (Revelation 1:4, 9-11; NIV).

Thus, in a matter-of-fact way, John began his letter to the seven churches in Asia. There was nothing in his salutation to suggest that he was preparing to tell them a story so fantastic and so

17

hair-raising as to make modern-day science fiction seem like a fairy tale.

In the vision that John went on to describe, we see a Christ far different from the meek, mild Man from Nazareth who walked the shores of the Sea of Galilee healing the sick and teaching the brotherhood of man. Here we see a triumphant Christ, a victorious Christ, an eternal Christ—standing in the midst of seven candlesticks, which represent the seven churches to whom the message was addressed. He was clothed in a long, kingly robe with a golden girdle around His breast—His hair like snow-white wool and His eyes blazing like fire. He stood as the mighty conqueror, the living essence of the almighty and eternal God!

When John saw this glorious One, he fell at His feet as though dead. But as ever, gentle and reassuring, Christ laid His hand on John's head and said, "Do not be afraid. I am the first and the last, the living one. I am he who was dead, and now you see me alive for timeless ages! I hold in my hand the keys of death and the grave" (Revelation 1:17, 18; *Phillips*).

Then came the command to John to write down what he had seen, as Christ began His message to the churches. The time was growing short. The day of God's judgment upon the earth was drawing near. These churches—His own body on earth— had to be warned. They had to have time to repent. They had to be ready!

As we shall see, the messages followed a basic pattern. Christ began by acknowledging the churches' good works, by reproving them for their failure in some areas, by exhorting them to repentance, and by ending with a promise.

REMEMBER!

The church at Ephesus had a dynamic beginning. Paul started the Ephesian church, which became the Christian capital of Asia. The problem was that the people had lost their primary love of Jesus Christ. Their freshness and enthusiasm were gone; the power of their original experience was no longer there. The Ephesians were alienated and estranged from God. They were living a double life. They had become hypocritical.

Thus, while Christ commended their works, their labor, and their patience, He also rebuked their lost love, exhorted them to remember their beginning, and challenged them to do their first works over. Finally, He promised them, "To him that overcometh will I give to eat of the tree of life, which is in the midst of the paradise of God." The very tree of life whose fruit was denied to Adam and Eve will be given as nourishment to the overcomer. What a promise! (Read Revelation 2:2-5, 7.)

FEAR NOT!

The Christians of Smyrna were poor and severely persecuted—poor, because they were plundered and deprived of their right to work. Yet, even though these saints were poverty-stricken and destitute of the necesities of life, they were rich in the Spirit, having their treasures laid up in heaven.

To add to their misery, some were cast into prison. They were beaten and killed. They were put to death by sword, fire, crucifixion, and wild beasts.

No fault was leveled against this poor but faithful church. To them Christ exhorted: "Fear not!

19

ful!" To them Christ gave the promise: "He that overcometh shall not be hurt of the second death." The second death is the eternal death, the ever-burning lake of fire, the future abode of the wicked. (Read Revelation 2:9-11.)

BE HOLY!

Pergamos was a wealthy city, a cultural center. It had medical centers and a library second only to that of Alexander the Great. It was modern and up-to-date—a present-day New York, Chicago, or Los Angeles. It was also the seat of Satan! As Jerusalem was the holy city of God, so Pergamos was the city of Satan—one of the earliest centers of occult teaching and practices. In Pergamos alongside the temples dedicated to the gods were temples devoted to the emperor. A Christian living in Pergamos knew quite well that his acceptance of Christ automatically made him liable for death. There was a law that once a year every Roman citizen should go to the temple of the emperor, burn a pinch of incense, and say, "Caesar is Lord." Having done this, the citizen was given a written certificate to prove that he had made this act of worship. Having so confessed, the Roman citizen could worship any god he chose so long as that worship did not conflict with public decency.

Consequently, a class of Christians arose who were willing to demonstrate their Christianity in Christian circles, but who were equally prepared to play down their Christianity in circles where Christianity was met with ridicule. They were willing to compromise their beliefs. How often have you heard the statement: "Sure we're Christians, but everyone else does it. Do you want us to stick out like a sore thumb? We don't want to be called fanatics!" Christ's message to this church was, "Stop your loose living. Be ye holy as I am holy, and I will fill you with 'hidden manna' and give you a 'white stone,' symbolic of pardon." (Read Revelation 2:13-17.)

CHOOSE!

Thyatira was a trade center. Guilds and unions were located there, and it flourished as a hub of commercial activity. Dyers, weavers, tanners, tentmakers, and skilled artisans of all kinds practiced their trades there. But there was a problem. A false prophetess named Jezebel was deceiving many with her false doctrines. She insisted there was no harm in accepting the world's customs and the world's ways. In effect, she was saying that if the standards of the Word of God clashed with business interests, then the standards of God in those instances had to be abandoned. She saw nothing wrong with playing at religion and compartmentalizing—keeping the things of God for Sunday, then the rest of the week exercising "business as usual."

In a book by Charles M. Sheldon, *In His Steps,* the pastor of a large and wealthy congregation challenged his people to try an experiment. For one year they were to ask themselves before making any major decision, "What would Jesus do?" Then, each one was to follow Jesus as exactly as he knew how, regardless of what the results might be. The effect was astonishing: A newspaper almost went out of business because the editor suddenly canceled all advertisements for cigarettes, alcohol, and objectionable entertainment. A railroad company execu-

21

tive found his position jeopardized when he accidentally came into some highly confidential information. A beautiful young singer passed up a lucrative offer to sing in public because she felt Jesus would not have her use her talents for financial and social success. Each individual who participated found himself deeply involved in a struggle: trying to weigh the standards of the world against the standards of Jesus Christ.

The Christians at Thyatira couldn't filter out this kind of living. They were having a hard time making the decision. But to those who remained faithful to Him, Christ promised not to place any other burden upon them and exhorted them to hold fast until His coming. The overcoming saints were promised (1) authority over the nations (during the reign of Christ on earth they will reign with Him as kings and priests) and (2) the morning star (they will be with Christ, who is the bright and morning star standing among the seven churches). Peter warned in 2 Peter 1:19, "Whereunto ye do well that ye take heed, as unto a light that shineth in a dark place, until the day dawn, and the day star arise in your hearts." (Read Revelation 2:19-28.)

BE REAL!

This church had a name. She had a good reputation and appeared to be alive to human eyes; yet God, who sees the inner spirit, declared her to be dead. The Spirit's piercing look saw the inward deadness of this church despite her outward busyness. The Lord reminded this church that He would

22

come at an hour they knew not. Some had already perished in the Sardis church, and those that remained were warned that unless they repented, they would also perish. They had received the true message of the Lord. His servant John was the founder of this church. Now they were being exhorted by this same John to remember the words of the Lord Jesus, who said that He would come as a thief in the night.

Within the church at Sardis, however, were some members who had remained faithful and who had distinguished themselves in so doing. We can imagine that there were men of the caliber of Martin Luther, John Wycliffe, and other giants of the Christian faith who worked diligently to preserve the teachings John had given them. Even though their names are lost to us, we may be sure they are written in "the Lamb's book of life" (Revelation 21:27) and that we will find them "clothed in white raiment" around the throne of the most holy God. (Read Revelation 3:1-5.)

STAND FAST!

When a church remains faithful as Philadelphia did, it does not necessarily follow that her reward will be a flowery bed of ease. This church was given a further work to do. Not only was the road that passed Philadelphia a main route for the imperial postal service, but caravans of merchants and the great armies of Caesar traveled along that highway. What a missionary opportunity was afforded those faithful Philadelphians!

After the days of John, Philadelphia was to go through great trials; but she kept the Word. And because this church kept faith with God she was promised that she would be kept from the Great Tribulation, which would come upon all the world. These people had patience and strength. They had not denied the name of their God; therefore, they would stand stalwart—sturdy, valiant, and resolute—as pillars in the temple of the most high God. (Read Revelation 3:8-12.) *Church*

REPENT!

Laodicea

It is interesting to note that Laodicea had the dubious distinction of being the only church of which Christ had nothing good to say. Ancient Laodicea was one of the wealthiest cities in the world. In fact, it was so wealthy that it "did not even need" God. Can you compare Laodicea's position with that of America today? Look at the wealth of this country. In 1933, fewer than half of the American families earned as much as $5,000 a year. Today we find that 76 percent earn more than $5,000; 36 percent, more than $10,000. Two out of three of today's families own or are buying a house. The State of California alone has more automobiles than either England or France. Many Americans pride themselves on their self-sufficiency. Laodicea was a self-sufficient city. Upon being ravaged in A.D. 61 by an earthquake, the city restored itself completely without government aid. Medicine, eye ointment, wool, manufacturing, and banking brought fame to Laodicea. Note how Christ, the perfect teacher, related His message to these products and occupations.

His accusation toward this city was that it was

totally indifferent to the things of God. Christ said, "He that is not with me is against me: and he that gathereth not with me scattereth" (Luke 11:23). Neutrality and unconcern are intolerable. If you can imagine a bowl of lukewarm oatmeal, you can get a fair picture of the indignation and revulsion God must have felt toward these people. Nonetheless, the door was not closed even to them. In loving grace and mercy, Jesus assured them that He was standing even yet at the door and knocking. Repentance could be theirs if they would only open the door and invite Him in. (Read Revelation 3:15-21.)

Well, this is all very interesting, I suppose, but what has it to do with us? Why should messages to churches that existed almost two thousand years ago be of any concern to us?

The Bible is a contemporary book. The strengths and weaknesses enumerated in the letter to these ancient churches are the same strengths and weaknesses that exist today in our churches and in our individual lives. We, too, need to remember from whence we are fallen and to regain our lost love. We, too, need to stop our loose living and to be holy. We, too, must choose whom we will serve. And we, too, must learn to be real!

Christ's messages to His churches in Asia are His messages to us as well. We must heed the warning: "The night is far spent, the day is at hand: let us therefore cast off the works of darkness, and let us put on the armour of light" (Romans 13:12).

"He that hath an ear, let him hear what the Spirit saith unto the churches!"

3

A LOOK AT THE THRONE

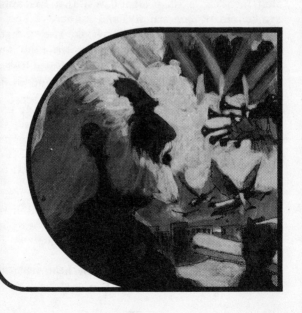

With the beginning of chapter 4 in the book of Revelation, the scene moves from earth to heaven. John was caught up in the Spirit and admitted to the throne room of the living God. The throne and the One who sits on it are the center of all activity in heaven.

The word *throne* is used 173 times in the Bible and forty times in Revelation alone. From its earliest mention to its present-day use, it has always symbolized power, majesty, and authority. The Bible does not tell us much about the material construction of this throne; and although John must have seen it in his vision, he did not describe it. Rather, he emphasized its grandeur, majesty, and dominion.

Although God's throne is referred to many times in the Bible, this is the first recorded instance that man was given a look at the kinds of things that go on around the throne of God. It's as if God, through John, were unveiling a part of Himself never before revealed. Now, through the opened door we catch a glimpse of what we will participate in as His children.

THE DOOR INTO HEAVEN

As John peered through this door, the first thing that he was made aware of was that God is real.

God is not some figment of man's imagination. He is a very real presence—awesome, majestic, powerful. He controls the events of earth, and He maintains the order of the universe from His seat on the throne. He gave John the unprecedented privilege of entering into His presence.

John's entrance through the door is comparable to the Rapture. What's the Rapture? The word *rapture* means "a catching away" or "a lifting up." It is not used in the New Testament, but it graphically describes what we as Christians will experience when Christ comes for His people and is described in 1 Thessalonians 4:16, 17.

However preposterous it may sound to us, the Bible clearly and emphatically states that this is what is going to take place. (Read 1 Corinthians 15:51, 52.)

Most of us have watched the launching of a spaceship. We've waited tensely during the countdown and watched the seconds tick by on our television screens. Finally comes the blast-off, when the ship ponderously lifts off the launching pad. We watch with expectancy as it lifts higher and higher, gaining speed all the time, until finally it becomes a blip on our screen and then disappears.

What an exhilarating experience for the astronauts inside! What a technological achievement! But the space trip of the astronauts is nothing compared to the space trip you and I will take when Jesus comes for those who belong to Him. No space suits, no spaceship, no rockets! In the "twinkling of an eye" (1 Corinthians 15:52), which is one thousandth of a second, we will be translated from earth past the moon, stars, and sun, through the heavenly door, and into the presence of God. Our minds simply cannot take in the momentousness of this event. Hundreds of thousands of people will just disappear from earth. Can you imagine it? You say, "What about all the people who will be left on earth?" We'll see what happens to them in a later chapter as we continue through the book of Revelation.

How do you get to go in the Rapture? What do you do? Do you go through some kind of ritual? Do you follow some type of formula? The Bible gives nine qualifications for those who will go in the Rapture:

1. *Be "Christ's."* Belong to Him; be His child (1 Corinthians 15:23; Galatians 5:24).
2. *Be "in Christ."* This is our position before God. We are accepted in Christ because of His sacrificial death for our sins (1 Thessalonians 4:16, 17; 2 Corinthians 5:17; Ephesians 1:3, 4).
3. *Be "blessed and holy."* Be undefiled by the world (Revelation 20:4-6).
4. *Be "good."* Endeavor to live by Christ's example (John 5:28, 29).
5. *Be in "the way, the truth, and the life."* Recognize that the only way to God is through His Son, Jesus Christ (John 14:1-6).
6. *Be "worthy."* Don't be careless or negligent; be alert and watchful for His coming (Luke 21:34-36).
7. *Be in "the church" or "body of Christ."* Be a part of the church where Christ is the head and the members are the body (Ephesians 5:

27; 1 Corinthians 12:13; Ephesians 1:22, 23; Colossians 1:18-24).

8. *Be pure, "even as he is pure."* Subjugate the inclinations of your evil nature (1 John 3:2, 3; 2 Corinthians 7:1; Galatians 5:16-24; Hebrews 12:14).

9. *Be without "spot, or wrinkle . . . and without blemish."* Be clean and spotless, having had all the stains of sin removed by Jesus' blood (Ephesians 5:27).

If we have accepted Christ as our personal Savior and are living according to the guidelines above, then we can look forward to being among those who will one day take that incredible space flight.

So, to show us something of what it's going to be like when we get there, God gave John an invitation and said to him, "Come up here, and I will show you what must take place in the future" (Revelation 4:1; *Amplified*). Let's take a look at what John saw.

THE THRONE IN HEAVEN

Much more important than any throne is the person who sits on that throne! Many thrones through the ages have been graced with the dignity and splendor of their rulers, but none can in any way compare with the throne on which sits the triune God—Father, Son, and Holy Spirit.

When John looked at it, he said it was a blur of brilliant light like the dazzling brightness of precious stones. He saw in it the clear transparency of the jasper and the beautiful, bright red of the sardine.

Surrounding the throne was a green—almost emerald—rainbow. The rainbow symbolizes the covenant God made with man never again to destroy the earth as He did at the Flood. (See Genesis 9:11-17.) This heavenly rainbow seems to tell us that although terrible things are going to happen to the earth and many disasters will occur, God will keep His covenant and will not destroy it completely. Some people believe that the earth will blow up and pass into oblivion, but the presence of the rainbow around the throne denies this. Green is the color of nature; and since creation, season after season, nature has reproduced itself. Each spring as the little buds form on the branches and the first green leaves push their way out, we are filled with a sense of promise and hope. It is this sense of promise and hope that is conveyed by the rainbow around the throne. So while the jasper and sardine may signify the awesome power and glory of God's character and His capacity to bring judgment on the world, the soft green of the rainbow reflects His immutability and the steadfastness of His Word. What God says He will do, He'll do. Surrounding God, then, is the majesty of His created color, the brilliance of His created light, and the glory of His eternal power. There's just no way we can really picture this.

A young girl who had been blind from birth was told that with the increase in medical knowledge an operation could possibly restore her sight. For fourteen years her mother had been her eyes. She had described the beauty of a sunset, the glory of a sunrise, the majesty of clouds, the darkness of a storm, and the redness of a robin's breast and had tried to give word pictures of what nature and creation were all about. The operation was performed, and everyone waited anxiously through the healing period. Finally the day came when the surgeon was to remove the bandages. The hospital staff gathered with the girl's mother around the bed as the doctor gently pulled back the bandages one by one. Tensely they waited as the final covering was removed. The girl sat up in bed, happened to glance out the window, and saw the sun shining brightly in a clear, blue sky; she saw the lush green of the trees and the lawn, and spotted the birds flitting through the air. Suddenly she clasped her hands together, ran to the window, looked out wide-eyed, and exclaimed, "Oh, Mother, why didn't you tell me it was so beautiful?" We can try to imagine what the One who sits on the throne of God is like, but we will have to wait until the "bandages" are removed from our mortal eyes before we really comprehend the glory, power, and majesty of the living God.

Not only was there light coming from the throne of God, but there was sound too. John wrote, "And out of the throne proceeded lightnings and thunderings and voices: and there were seven lamps of fire burning before the throne, which are the seven Spirits of God" (Revelation 4:5). The seven spirits of God mentioned here depict the full work of the Holy Spirit. It is the Holy Spirit who touches our hearts and brings us into a new relationship with God. These seven spirits show us the broad scope of the Holy Spirit's ministry, which touches every aspect of our lives.

In front of the throne John saw a glassy sea like crystal, which was the actual floor of the throne room. Have you ever seen a sea or a lake when it was so calm that it looked like glass? Not one ripple stirred the water. Thus, we see, God revealed another aspect of His character here—His calmness. There were thunderings and lightnings around the throne, and the world was about to be plunged into a violent conflict, such as it had never known, when John saw the awesome scene; yet in the midst of all this was the calmness of God. Yes, God is in control, regardless.

There's something else we can learn here, too. In Exodus 24:9-11 the Bible refers to the fact that Moses, Aaron, Nadab, Abihu, and the seventy elders of Israel actually saw God standing on "as it were a paved work of a sapphire stone, and as it were the body of heaven in his clearness" (verse 10). This reveals to us that the glassy sea John saw was not actually a sea like we know one to be, but a hard, flat, transparent surface. This is another indication that heaven is not a nebulous place of shadows, but is substantial and real, just as God is substantial and real.

THE WORSHIPERS IN HEAVEN

In the next scene John saw twenty-four elders seated around the throne. Who were these elders? How did they get there? Whom did they represent?

These twenty-four elders are a characterization of the church of the Lord Jesus Christ, which is comprised of all those who have accepted His way of salvation. We know they're not angels, because John saw them wearing crowns and dressed in white garments. The Bible refers several times to crowns, thrones, and white garments, and in each case the recipients of these rewards are the Chris-

33

tians who have overcome the evil powers of this world.

How did these elders get to heaven? The only way would have been the Rapture. Somewhere between Revelation chapter 3 and chapter 4, we read, the rapture of the Church will take place, and all those who belong to Christ will be ushered into God's presence. It's interesting to note that after chapter 3 in the book of Revelation the Church is never referred to again until we come to chapter 19. During this time sequence the church of the Lord Jesus will be at rest in His presence.

Why twenty-four elders? What's the significance of the number? Although no specific answer is given, we are told in 1 Chronicles 24:1-19 that the whole priesthood in the Old Testament was represented by twenty-four elders and that their job was to minister in the Temple as God had instructed them. Also, it is believed that the twenty-four elders depict the twelve tribes of Israel and the twelve apostles, since Revelation 21:12-14 tell us that these names will be written on the gates and the foundation stones of the New Jerusalem, which God will build after all His terrible judgments are over.

So, now we can see how these elders represent all the teeming millions who will meet around the throne of God. All those who lived in Old Testament times who were saved through faith in God, while waiting expectantly for the perfect Passover Lamb, the Messiah, will be there. People who lived and died during the Church Age—that period of time from after Christ's resurrection until the Rapture—will be there. They will be the ones who have accepted Jesus Christ as their personal Savior

34

and either have died and have been resurrected or have been caught up in the Rapture. Also, 144,000 Jews and a countless multitude of people, who will be saved during the period of God's terrible judgments, will be there.

What a tremendous gathering! Imagine the biggest crowd you've ever seen—then multiply it thousands of times. All these myriads of people will unite together to give praise and glory to God. Do you know what it means to be united in spirit? It means to be on the same wavelength.

This unity is illustrated by the excitement of a crucial football game. Imagine the players in their second overtime period; the game, still tied. Suddenly one player completes a pass, breaks loose, and heads for the end zone. Spontaneously and simultaneously the crowd stands to its feet and roars its encouragement. It is obvious that they are many, yet they are one in spirit. And yet this is nothing compared to the unity of spirit to be experienced by all who will one day gather around the throne of God to worship the triune God, lifting their voices as one in praise to Him!

THE OFFICIALS OF HEAVEN

After this John's attention was turned to four strange-looking creatures. He described them as having different features, but said that all of them were covered with eyes and had wings. Some translators of the Bible have unfortunately used the word *beasts* as the English equivalent, but the word in the original Greek should be translated "living creatures." These were not beasts as we imagine from our horror programs, but living creatures created by God for specific purposes. They were His official messengers and attendants who were assigned particular errands and duties.

Let's take a closer look at these strange creatures. Each one had a different appearance. The first one looked like a lion and indicated the characteristics of courage and kingliness. The second one looked like the calf of an ox. In John's day the ox was an important part of life. There were no machines to grind grain, no tractors to plow fields, and no semis to transport goods cross-country. People came to depend on the ox for many things. It's easy to see the characteristics represented here—patience, strength, endurance, and perseverance. The third had the face of a man. Man is the highest form of God's creation; he has the intelligence, personality, and emotional makeup lacking in the animal world. The fourth living creature was like a flying eagle, depicting the piercing vision, soaring power, and high aspirations of this magnificent bird.

It is interesting to look back into the Old Testament and to see how these same figures were used in the camping and marching order of Israel through the Wilderness. When they came to a rest site, the Tabernacle would be placed in the middle of the area. The camp of Judah, with Issachar and Zebulun, would rest on the east side around a banner bearing the figure of a lion. The camp of Ephraim, with Manasseh and Benjamin, would rest on the west around a banner bearing the figure of an ox. The camp of Reuben, with Simeon and Gad, would rest on the south around its banner bearing the figure of a man. The camp of Dan, with Asher and Naphtali, would rest on the south around its banner bearing the figure of an eagle. So the Tabernacle, the place of God's presence, was surrounded and protected at all times. The emblems on these banners were symbols of the divine power that led, guided, and protected the children of Israel as they marched out of bondage, wandered through the Wilderness, and finally settled in the Promised Land. As a parallel, the function of the living creatures John saw in heaven was also to surround and guard the new camp of the Lord which, eventually, would comprise the whole world.

These living creatures also had wings. These wings enabled them to move rapidly to do God's wishes. They also had eyes in front, behind, and within. These eyes symbolized the ability to look back into the past, forward into the future, and inward to themselves. These living creatures were supremely equipped to administer God's kingdom with insight, perception, and judiciousness.

We now have the whole scene before us: In the center is the throne of Almighty God in all its glory and brilliance. Surrounding it is the rainbow. In front is the glassy sea. Gathered around the throne are the twenty-four elders representing all the redeemed of all ages. Burning before the throne are the seven lamps of fire representing the seven spirits of God. In the midst and round the throne are the four living creatures who never rest from worshiping God. The living creatures and all the myriads of people around the throne unite together in praise and adoration to the One who is worthy to receive such praise. In one spirit they bow before Him and say:

> Thou art worthy, O Lord, to receive glory and honour and power: for thou hast created all things, and for thy pleasure they are and were created (Revelation 4:11).

q

THE
SEVEN-SEALED
BOOK

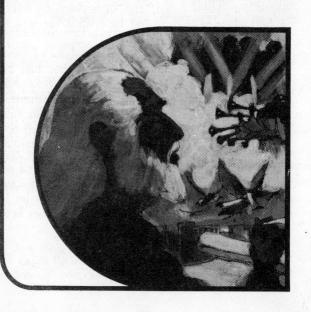

Naomi and her daughter-in-law Ruth arrived back in Bethlehem one day feeling tired, sad, and dispirited. Naomi had left her home country years before and had moved to Moab to escape the famine in the land. While she was there, her husband and her sons died. Although a Gentile Moabitess, Ruth would not leave her mother-in-law, whom she dearly loved, and so decided to return to Bethlehem with her and face whatever was in store.

Upon arrival back in the Promised Land, Naomi found that the home and land that had belonged to her husband had been confiscated, probably due to debts. She and Ruth were penniless. To get food to eat, Ruth went to glean in the field of Boaz, a wealthy landowner who, it turned out, was a relative of her deceased husband, Mahlon. Boaz became interested in Ruth and Naomi's plight and took the matter to the local authorities. Under Levitical law Boaz was eligible to win back the lands of his relative if he could meet three requirements:

1. He had to be the next of kin.
2. He had to be willing.
3. He had to be able; that is, he had to have the money available.

39

The legal papers from the deal confiscating the land were always written on two scrolls. One was signed on the back by witnesses and posted in the Temple for all to read as they wished. The second was sealed with seven seals and was only brought out when the relative gave evidence that he was willing and able to buy back the land. So Boaz went to the judge and, upon proving that he fulfilled the requirements, was able to hand back to Naomi the land and home she had lost.

The relationship of Boaz to Naomi, and his willingness and ability to win back her property, coupled with the signing and sealing of the scrolls, will help us to understand more clearly what John described in Revelation chapters 5 and 6.

Chapter 5 of the book of Revelation opens with John's attention being focused on the scroll or book in God's hand and the seven seals on it. He heard a loud voice crying out, "Who is worthy to open the book, and to loose the seals thereof?" (Revelation 5:2).

It seems as though the whole of heaven paused breathlessly as those around the throne waited for someone to step forward—but no one did. So John began to weep deep, racking sobs of disappointment as he realized the implications of the situation. If no one could be found to open the book, then man would forever be separated from his inheritance and God's promise would not be fulfilled.

Then one of the elders spoke to him, saying, "Do not weep. See, the lion from the tribe of Judah, the root of David, has won the victory and is able to open the book and break its seven seals" (Revelation 5:5; *Phillips*). As his eyes cleared, he saw in the center of the throne a Lamb that seemed to have been slaughtered. He had seven horns and seven eyes, again depicting the sevenfold ministry of the Holy Spirit. The Lamb then took the book from the right hand of the One on the throne. Suddenly a thrill of joy went through all those around the throne. They broke into a new song:

Worthy art thou to take the book and break its seals, for thou hast been slain and by thy blood hast purchased for God men from every tribe, and tongue, and people, and nation! Thou hast made them a kingdom of priests for our God, and they shall reign as kings upon the earth (Revelation 5: 9, 10; *Phillips*).

Jesus Christ, God's Son (He was our "next of kin") by His coming to earth as a man and dying on the cross (He was willing) paid the price with His blood (He was able). Jesus redeemed our inheritance so that we could one day come into what is rightfully ours—to reign as kings upon the earth once again.

Then John heard this heavenly song picked up and echoed by the hosts of heaven—countless myriads of people purchased with the blood of the Lamb—and together they joined in to give honor and glory and blessing to the One who was worthy! They joined in praise too because now the seals could be broken and God's countdown toward the end of the age could begin.

The end of the age, as John saw it, has not yet come to pass. When it does, it will culminate in the personal, visible return of Jesus Christ to establish the kingdom of God on earth. The opening of the seals will begin a seven-year period of great suffering, distress, affliction, and trial referred to as the Tribulation. These seven years will be the most fateful in all human history. Jesus Himself said that if He didn't return to earth to end the Tribulation, no one would be left alive. (See Matthew 24:22.) None of the wars, earthquakes, famines, and other disasters that have occurred before come close to comparing with what is in store for the world. During this period God will allow sin to run its tragic course. He will lift His restraining and controlling hand from all creation, and horrors worse than what the wildest imagination of man could ever dream up will be permitted to take place.

Why will God do this? Primarily God will be concerned with the nation of Israel, His chosen people, and these judgments will deal with Israel and bring them to the place where they will acknowledge Jesus Christ—the One whom they rejected and crucified—as their Messiah. God's desire will be to bring them to complete repentance and to purify the nation.

During this Tribulation period God will send troubles and calamities on Israel to take out all the rebelliousness toward God that has been characteristic of this nation down through history.

"So," you ask, "why will the rest of the world have to suffer if God will be dealing primarily with Israel?"

The Jewish nation has suffered unspeakable horrors at the hands of other nations. In World War II alone some six million Jews were methodically searched out, hunted down, and killed by the Nazis. Even today nations are acting against the Jews. On November 10, 1975, a resolution was passed by the General Assembly of the United Nations equating Zionism (Jewish national life) with racism and denouncing Israel. Now it's God's time to punish the nations for their persecution of His people.

This Tribulation time will also constitute Satan's last fling on earth before the Millennial reign. Since the time of Adam, Satan has had freedom on earth. During these last days, however, his time is running short; he knows that God will one day take from him all authority over the earth and give it back to man. So during the Tribulation period he will work frantically to prevent people from becoming reconciled to God. The first thing he will do is shown to us by the breaking of the first seal.

SEAL NUMBER ONE: WORLD RULER

As John watched the activities in heaven, he saw the worthy One open the first seal. He then heard one of the living creatures say "Come and see." And John saw a rider on a white horse. This rider was then instructed to go out and begin his campaign to conquer the nations of the earth. This was the signal for the action to begin.

Who will this rider on the white horse be? In the Bible this man is referred to as the Antichrist. And that is just what he will be—the complete opposite to everything Christ is and stands for. The Antichrist will be a fake; people won't recognize him for what he really is, because above all he will be a deceiver. He'll show to them only his good side; they'll see the leadership abilities of a President, the diplomacy of a statesman, the personal magnetism of a rock superstar, the brilliant mind of a genius. What they won't see until it is too late will be his Satan-controlled nature. It is this man, then, who will skillfully, subtly, and relentlessly pursue his plan to become world ruler.

Revelation 6:2 says he will carry a bow, but Scripture makes no mention of any arrow to go with the bow. The inference here is that this man will conquer the world by persuasion rather than by force. He will come with the answers to the world's political, economic, and social problems and the world will fall at his feet in gratitude.

SEAL NUMBER TWO: WAR!

As the worthy One opened the second seal, the second living creature again called upon John to "come and see." As John looked, he saw another rider, only this time he came on a red horse. This rider was given the power to shatter the pseudo-peace on the earth and to begin a war that will escalate into the greatest battle in the history of mankind. Russia and her allies (the Arab nations, Iran, and Germany) will attack Israel for the purpose of claiming the tremendous mineral wealth lying untapped in the Dead Sea. It is estimated that there is enough potash there to supply the needs of the world for two thousand years.

"So who wants potash?" you ask.

Potash is extremely valuable for two reasons:
1. It is used in fertilizer. In a world where food becomes increasingly hard to obtain, potash represents a life-giving property.
2. It is also used in explosives. We know the implications of this.

Kirban states: "It has been estimated that the value of potash, bromine, and other chemical salts in the Dead Sea is 1 trillion, 270 billion dollars!"

44

(Salem Kiban, *Kirban's Prophecy New Testament,* p. 149). No wonder Russia will want to gain control of this territory!

SEAL NUMBER THREE: FAMINE!

Famine was symbolized by the rider on the black horse, carrying a pair of scales. In the days before our modern packaging methods, grain, sugar, flour, etc. were measured out on scales. The Scriptures tell us that after this judgment comes on the earth, it will take a whole day's wages for a man to buy food for himself and his family.

In spite of birth control programs and increased technology on methods of growing food, the population is multiplying faster than the world can produce the food to feed it! We have all seen pictures of the starving millions in India, Asia, and Africa who don't know what it's like *not* to feel hungry. Imagine it: a perpetual gnawing inside of you that never goes away! This is what will spread across the world as the result of the exploding population and the collapse of economic stability.

SEAL NUMBER FOUR: DEATH!

Following closely on the heels of the second and third riders was the fourth, representing Death. The pale color referred to was actually a sickly green, the color of decaying and dying tissue. His coming so closely on the heels of Famine constituted a logical sequence of events. After war and famine what do you get? Death. Because of the tremendous scope of the previous two judgments, millions of people will die. Death will be given dominion over one-fourth of the earth. Trailing after Death is Hades, who will gather up the victims into the "unseen world."

These Four Horsemen of the Apocalypse, as they are called, will continue to ride during the remainder of the Tribulation period.

SEAL NUMBER FIVE: MARTYRDOM OF BELIEVERS

The fifth seal depicted the persecution and martyrdom of those who believe in Christ. There are many people today who know that Christ will someday come for His people in the Rapture. They've read about it. They've heard it preached. But they are not prepared to make the commitment necessary so that they will be ready for Him when He comes.

These people, then, during the Tribulation, will be well aware of what is going on in the world. Many will turn to God, but they will pay a terrible price. At this time things on earth will begin to go awry. The world ruler will not come through like he promised, and horrible misfortunes and disasters will occur. Nonbelievers will wonder what is going on. "Who's to blame for all this?" they will ask themselves. Instead of looking at themselves, they will look around for someone to blame. "It's the Christians!" they will say. "It's their fault!" And so they will kill all those who claim to know Christ. The Bible tells us that a great multitude of Tribulation saints will pay the supreme price for their faith.

SEAL NUMBER SIX: CREATION SHAKEN

The sixth seal released violent disturbances on the earth and in the air. The word used was *earthquake,* but more than earth will be affected. It will be as if the universe is jolted and jarred until everything slides from its place. Some people believe that this great commotion could easily fit the description of a nuclear explosion: the violent shaking of earth, the light of the sun being blocked out, the moon appearing to be red through the contaminated atmosphere, and meteors and space junk blazing through the air and appearing like stars. Knowing what we now know about nuclear explosions, it is quite easy to see how John's vision could come to pass through man-made devices.

Further, rulers and the servants, the wealthy and the destitute, and all those in-between will run frantically to find shelter in caves and under huge rocks. They will recognize that they are experiencing the judgments of God almighty. However, instead of calling on Him for mercy, they will call on the rocks to fall on them and hide them from the wrath of God. Man will still be running away from God. It will take man many more horrifying judgments before he will acknowledge God's sovereignty and will bow to His Son, Jesus Christ.

SEAL NUMBER SEVEN: SILENCE

Then, when he had broken the seventh seal, there was utter silence in Heaven for what seemed to me half an hour (Revelation 8:1; *Phillips*).

As John looked, the thunder stopped rolling, the lightning stopped flashing, the heavenly choir was silent. A breathless hush fell on everyone around the throne. An atmosphere of awe and trepidation permeated the surroundings.

Thus, the time will have come to advance God's clock a little further; and as they look into the future and see the fearful things still to take place, the whole of heaven will become mute and silent.

47

5

ISRAEL
RISES AGAIN

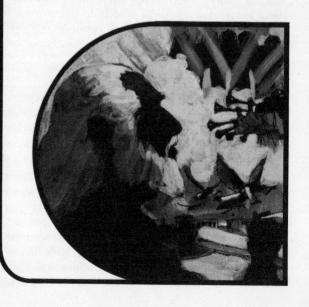

If you have ever been homesick, no doubt you remember that aching loneliness, that strange lump in the throat, that steady fighting to hold back the tears. Maybe it was your first day at school or your first summer youth camp. Or maybe it was just spending the night away from home for the first time and seeing out the window twinkling lights that reminded you of home.

For more than 1,900 years the nation of Israel had lived in bondage far from home. In a sense they were homesick. Memories of Jerusalem and the Promised Land had been passed down from generation to generation, and the oft-repeated phrase "next year in Jerusalem" had become not only a watchword but a hopeful prayer.

And so rich and poor, old and young, they began gathering back—no doubt hopeful. Yet when they did, they found no welcome mat awaiting their return.

While the Jews had been scattered from one corner of the earth to the other, the Arab nations —descendants of Ishmael, Abraham's son by the servant girl Hagar—had occupied the land. Further, they had cultivated the friendship of the British who had been given a mandate over the land of Palestine by the League of Nations.

Therefore, when the Jews began filtering into Palestine, the British imposed severe restrictions on Jewish immigration. They waylaid and held them in detention camps on the island of Cyprus— which were little better than the prison camps from which most of the Jewish refugees had come. Naturally the Jews were unhappy. However, the plight of these homeless Jews aroused the sympathies of much of the world. As a result, after World War II the United Nations agreed to a partition of Palestine into a Jewish state and an Arab state.

On May 15, 1948, the British withdrew control, and Israel proclaimed herself an independent state. But instead of her troubles being over, they were just beginning. The Arab nations refused to recognize Israel and denied her rights to existence. Before the day was out Israel was attacked by Egypt, Jordan, Iraq, Syria, Lebanon, and Saudi Arabia.

Subsequent hostilities followed in 1956 and led up to full-blown wars in 1967 and 1973. These wars, followed by uneasy truce agreements, motivated Israel to establish the most vigorous nation in the world. She was now aware that survival among the surrounding hostile nations would mean fateful and crucial conflict.

Already in this quarter we have seen that the Bible prophesied Israel's dispersion and regathering. We have noted Israel's struggles for survival in alien nations and ultimately the Jews restoration to the land of Palestine. Once again, we see, God's Word is proving itself to be infallible.

The return of the Jewish people and their establishment as a new state is significant in light of many Old Testament prophecies that are now being literally fulfilled. Equally significant is Israel's unparalleled establishment as a major military and political power.

Suddenly Scripture comes alive before our eyes (see Isaiah 61:4; Amos 9:14). Even now we hear the Prophet Ezekiel declare:

> Thus saith the Lord God; In the day that I shall have cleansed you from all your iniquities I will also cause you to dwell in the cities, and the wastes shall be builded. And the desolate land shall be tilled, whereas it lay desolate in the sight of all that passed by. And they shall say, This land that was desolate is become like the garden of Eden; and the waste and desolate and ruined cities are become fenced, and are inhabited. Then the heathen that are left round about you shall know that I the Lord build the ruined places, and plant that that was desolate: I the Lord have spoken it, and I will do it.
>
> Thus saith the Lord God; I will yet for this be enquired of by the house of Israel, to do it for them; I will increase them with men like a flock. As the holy flock, as the flock of Jerusalem in her solemn feasts; so shall the waste cities be filled with flocks of men: and they shall know that I am the Lord (Ezekiel 36:33-38).

Until 1948 the land of Israel had lain in a virtual state of waste for over 1,900 years. In A.D. 70-73 Israel was conquered and scattered by the Romans throughout the world until today (since 1948) over three million Jewish immigrants have returned to Israel, from over 102 different countries, representing some thirty-eight different languages.* For 1,900 years Israel lay dormant in rocks, sand dunes, barren hills, and rising dust. Today it literally blooms like a rose.

In just a few short years, under the providential guidance of Jehovah God, Israel has turned a wasteland into an Eden. The accomplishments read like an Old Testament account of inhabiting the original Promised Land, and in living color the sand dunes rise up to become fertile fields.

First, since 1948 over 160 million trees* have been planted, and once desolate mountains now form a green line which extends the length of the country.

Second, the water resources of Israel, although limited, have been utilized to miraculous proportions. The very heart of the country lies in one small pumping station located at the Sea of Galilee. From this station the fresh water of the Galilee is pumped from seven hundred feet below sea level eighteen miles uphill to Nazareth, which is 1,500 feet above sea level. From Nazareth the force of gravity is utilized to pull the life-giving water flow downward into the (semi) desert land of the Negev, the southern half of Israel, through a pipe that is eight feet in diameter. From this one major water source, supplemented by the Jordan River, occasional rainwater, and limited scattered wells, the fertile desert land has literally come alive. The beautiful Sea of Galilee, which is 17.5 miles long, 8 miles wide, and some 140 feet deep, now looms as God's gift to a green and prosperous Israel through an eight-foot pipe extending approximately 175* miles in length.

Third, agricultural and urban development have taken on new and limitless proportions.

For instance, in the ancient town and area of Hebron—the traditional burial place of Abraham, Isaac, and Jacob—the rocky hills are alive with trees, orchards, vineyards, and cultivation. Hebron was the spot where the spies of the Israelites first viewed the Promised Land and brought back the worried report of giants in the land and fortifications to the sky. Hebron was the city where David was anointed king as a political gesture to gain the favor and goodwill of the warlike and rugged Hebronites. Hebron was the place where the bombing of a tourist bus occurred in 1974, causing international repercussions. Today, however, Hebron shows relative calm and peace, with 37,000* Muslims and 3,000* Jews living together in an era of unprecedented agricultural activity on barren rocks and hillside slopes.

In the Negev the wastelands of sand and dust have taken on the richness of eucalyptus trees, pecan trees, cotton, and all varieties of vegetables and crops. At Beersheba, the place of Abraham's well and the general area where he and Lot divided to go their separate ways, one now sees a modern industrial city with factories and a booming metropolis. Beersheba is the capital of the Negev, and its present development literally fulfills Isaiah 61: 4, 5:

> And they shall build the old wastes, they shall raise up the former desolations, and they shall repair the waste cities, the desolations of many generations. And strangers shall stand and feed your flocks, and the sons of the alien shall be your plowmen and your vinedressers.

In 1948 there were only about three thousand Bedouins roaming the area of Beersheba. There

53

were no buildings except an old fort built by the Turks sometime between the fourth and seventh centuries. In 1950 the first Jewish family came in, and today 164,000* Jews live in a flourishing industrial city complete with television, modern transportation, and solar energy used for heating and cooling. In addition, some 400,000* Jews inhabit the deserts to the south, which lay abandoned and unoccupied for centuries.

In 1948 Ashkelon (in the Gaza Strip) was a little Arab Village and Egyptian army camp by the sea. Today it is a prospering city of 55,000* Jewish immigrants who have come from all over the world.

Since A.D. 70 no one had inhabited the ancient city of Ashdod, but in 1961 the first foundation of the first house was laid. In just fourteen years a city of approximately 40,000* Jewish refugees has been developed into a thriving seaport with oil refineries and factories; and there are plans to make it the most modern seaport in the world. It looks impossible and sounds incredible, but in the words of Moshe Tzur, "With God's help we are making the impossible possible."

In the Gaza Strip, virtually desolate since the first century, the words of Zephaniah 2:4-7 are actually coming alive.

On and on the story goes in Caesarea, Haifa, and Tel Aviv. Even in Jerusalem it is observed that just 120 years ago the first house was built outside of the old city walls; from 1967 until today over 80 percent of the now modern Jerusalem has been developed. In record time the City of David has taken its place in the world as a fully modern city and capital of the nation of Israel.

In this same regard the valley of Jezreel, the valley of Gog, where the Battles of Armageddon (Revelation 14:14-21; Ezekiel 39:17-24; Revelation 16:16; 19:19-20:3) will be fought, now stands out as one of the most fertile valleys in Israel. Covering an area measuring 18 by 22 miles, this valley was nothing but a swamp in 1922. The land had not been cultivated for about three thousand years. After being purchased in 1922 from Persia by the Zionist movement, a new day dawned for the valley of Jezreel, and today practically every inch of soil is productive.

The same story exists for the area around the Dead Sea, which now promises to become the Sea of Life. We all know about the Dead Sea. It is dead because it has no outlet. The high evaporation level takes out of it what the Jordan River pours in every day. The surface of the sea is 1,300 feet below sea level, and it is 1,300 feet at its deepest point. Sodom and Gomorrah once stood at the south end of this sea, but both were destroyed by the wrath of God and were submerged beneath the waters that formed the lowest and saltiest lake in the world. The Atlantic Ocean contains 3.2 percent salt; the Pacific Ocean, 3.6 percent; the Indian Ocean, 4.1 percent; the Red Sea, 4.2 percent; but the Dead Sea contains 33 percent salt together with 328 minerals. These minerals are looming in importance as magnesium, bromide, potash, potassium, and other minerals become necessary ingredients of fertilizer, metal alloys, and many other important products.

The phenomenal happening, however, is that today the Dead Sea miraculously is bordered by palm trees, banana plantations, and fields of strawberries, cucumbers, and eggplants. Further, for the first time in history freshwater ducks are landing near the Dead Sea. What a colossal occurrence— ducks at the Dead Sea!

Why should freshwater ducks stop at the world's saltiest lake? The answer is simple but complex. Fish hatcheries are going full blast to develop a new type of fish that can live in brackish water. If everything goes as planned, fishing lakes, filled with Dead Sea water that has been processed through special desalinization plants, will be stocked with these new fish.

New hotels are being built, beaches are being cleared of rocks, and the Dead Sea looks to a future of worldwide tourist trade for mineral baths, health spas, fishing, boating, swimming, and visits to historic Qumran and Masada. As one stands on the height of Masada (ancient fortress 1,300 feet above sea level) and looks over the blooming desert land of the Dead Sea and the present-day army camp of historic En-gedi (ancient site where David hid from Saul), Ezekiel 47:7-12 comes crashing through like a mighty crescendo from God:

> Now when I had returned, behold, at the bank of the river were very many trees on the one side and on the other. Then said he unto me, These waters issue out toward the east country, and go down into the desert, and go into the sea: which being brought forth into the sea, the waters shall be healed. And it shall come to pass, that every thing that liveth, which moveth, whithersoever the rivers shall come, shall live: and there shall be a very great multitude of fish, because these waters shall come thither: for they shall be healed; and every thing shall live whither the river cometh. And it shall come to pass, that the fishers shall stand upon it from En-gedi even unto En-eglaim; they shall be a

place to spread forth nets; their fish shall be according to their kinds, as the fish of the great sea, exceeding many. But the miry places thereof and the marishes thereof shall not be healed; they shall be given to salt. And by the river upon the bank thereof, on this side and on that side, shall grow all trees for meat, whose leaf shall not fade, neither shall the fruit thereof be consumed: it shall bring forth new fruit according to his months, because their waters they issued out of the sanctuary: and the fruit thereof shall be for meat, and the leaf thereof for medicine.

Fourth, a new spirit of cooperation seems to be emerging.

Obviously, Israel is a virtual melting pot of centuries of conflicting forces. In this one small country (approximately 60 miles wide and 280 miles* long) six religious cultures, including Jews, Muslims, Christians, Bahais, Hasidim, and Druses, are trying to learn to live in peace. Miraculously, at a grassroots level it is beginning to happen.

At Hebron Muslims and Jews share the same shrine for worship and celebration on their respective Sabbath days. In industry Arabs and Jews have come together in various corporate partnerships subsidized by government money. Even the centuries-old animosity between Jews and Samaritans is being wiped out, for in 1967 the chief rabbis of Israel recognized the Samaritans as complete Jews and permitted intermarriage between Jews and Samaritans. After 2,500 years of prejudice, isolation, and hostility the wall has been broken down to the point that many Samaritans have left their traditional land to become a vital part of Jewish life in the bustling city of Tel Aviv. In the Negev the centuries of unchanged Bedouin existence of tents, camels, goats, sheep, and endless wandering is giving way to modernized Bedouin villages complete with houses, schools, hospitals, and modern farming equipment. Even the Bedouin is caught up in this time of change. As further evidence of this new spirit of cooperation, the mayor of Jerusalem is an Arab; and Arabs are full-fledged citizens with full voting rights and privileges in Israeli governmental activities.

This new spirit may well be preparing the way for coalitions, agreements, and joint ventures with Arab countries, which, in turn, will open the door for an Antichrist takeover and unprecedented peace and prosperity in the first three and one-half years of the Tribulation.

As we return to our study of the book of Revelation, chapter 6, we see the sequence of events noted in the breaking of the seven seals. The scene of devastation and destruction that builds momentum here is without parallel in the history of the world.

For example, when the fourth seal is broken, one-fourth of the earth's population will be destroyed by death with the sword, famine, and wild beasts. If we apply this to the world's population, which is presently approaching three billion, it would mean that 750,000,000 people would perish! This is more than the total population of North America, South America, and Central America combined!

> *And after these things I saw four angels standing on the four corners of the earth, holding the four winds of the earth, that the wind should not blow on the earth, nor on the sea, nor on any tree. And*

I saw another angel ascending from the east, having the seal of the living God: and he cried with a loud voice to the four angels, to whom it was given to hurt the earth and the sea, Saying, Hurt not the earth, neither the sea, nor the trees, till we have sealed the servants of our God in their foreheads.

And I heard the number of them which were sealed: and there were sealed an hundred and forty and four thousand of all the tribes of the children of Israel (Revelation 7:1-4).

The Bible goes on to say that these 144,000 will sing a new song before God's throne, and no man can learn it but these 144,000. And who has a better right? These are Jewish men and women who have remained pure and true to their God. In the midst of a world gone totally away from God, they will have "follow[ed] the Lamb" (Revelation 14: 4). They will have followed Him through trial and persecution, and they will be graciously rewarded the opportunity to follow Him in glory!

Today, wherever we look in the nation of Israel, prophetic history is in the making. Teddy Kollek, mayor of Jerusalem, once remarked, "The Jews have prayed for Jerusalem for two thousand years." The Israeli Army's chief rabbi was moved when he said, "We have come home, never to be moved again— never!"

It is true! We see it fulfilled! Israel rises again, under the providential care of God. What Israel, even in her most believing fellowship, failed to realize, Jesus Christ has gloriously achieved and is fulfilling in the Kingdom work of His Spirit in this Church Age.

*Based on 1975 statistics.

6

THE SEVEN TRUMPETS

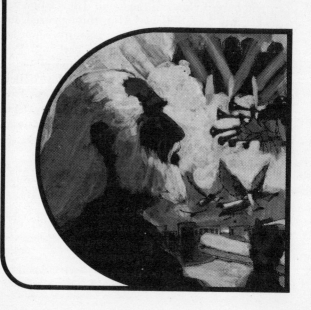

Many of the things that are described in the following chapters of Revelation may seem farfetched and fantastic. Nonetheless, just because they are fantastic to our understanding at this time does not mean that they cannot take place. Many things that seemed incredible and unimaginable years ago have become realities just since the turn of the century. Automobiles, air travel, space travel, mechanization, and computers, are a few examples.

Between the breaking of the first seal (Revelation 6:1, 2) and the seventh seal (Revelation 8: 1) almost three and a half years will pass. Terrible catastrophes will ravage the earth. Suffering will increase, but still man will not bow down to almighty God. His attitude will be that these calamities will pass, and the world will get better. However, such will not be the case.

According to John's narration in Revelation 8, seven angels will hold seven trumpets. These will be the highest ranking of God's angels, who stand "before God" as His generals or chiefs-of-staff. Their task will be to herald in the next stage of God's judgment on the earth.

But before they do this verse 3 says, "Another angel came and stood at the altar, having a golden

61

censer; and there was given unto him much incense, that he should offer it with the prayers of all saints upon the golden altar which was before the throne." It is believed that this other angel spoken of will be none other than Jesus Christ, who will assume His role of high priest and bear before the heavenly altar of God the prayers of all the saints down through the ages. He will then fill the censer from the fire of the altar and fling it toward earth. Thunderings, lightnings, and an earthquake will result. Jesus Himself will initiate the next phase of judgment on man.

Trumpets played a significant part in the history of the Jewish people. The blast of the trumpet called them to war or warned them when an enemy approached; the trumpet summoned them to meetings or indicated they were to march again; trumpets proclaimed festivals and feast days; the sound of a trumpet announced royalty. So it's no wonder that God will use trumpets to call attention to what will soon happen.

THE FIRST TRUMPET

The first angel will step forward; and at the sound of his trumpet, hail and fire mixed with blood will rain down upon earth (see Revelation 8:7). In Exodus 7:20 we read that God turned the water into blood. If God could do it then, He most certainly can do it again.

However, in this Nuclear Age in which we are living another possibility presents itself. Suppose there were to be a massive nuclear attack by one country on another. What would be the result?

Would it be something like this: "And the third part of trees was burnt up, and all green grass was burnt up" (Revelation 8:7)?

Someday, God says, one-third of all the trees on the earth and all grass will be destroyed. Remember, also, that during this part of the Tribulation a famine will still be going on. Think what the destruction of one-third of all trees and all grass will do to intensify food problems.

THE SECOND TRUMPET

As the second trumpet is sounded, a giant, blazing mass like a meteor or mountain will smash into the sea and one-third of the sea will be turned into blood. As this flaming mass hits the sea, one-third of all the living creatures in the sea will be destroyed.

How many nations live off the sea? Japan, Alaska, China, and the Scandinavian countries all have major fishing industries and rely heavily on fish for their daily diet.

So, now, not only will one-third of the land be destroyed, but a tremendous shortage of fish will develop. Thus, the famine will worsen.

What happens when you drop a rock into a bucket of water? The water plops over the side, doesn't it? Just so, another result from the impact of this blazing mass will be a giant tidal wave. Navy ships, merchant ships, giant tankers, small fishing vessels, stately passenger liners—whatever vessels are in the area—will be engulfed in the huge wall of water that will rise before them. One-third of the ships will be destroyed. (See Revelation

8:9). The result will be economic chaos, unbelievable famine conditions, and mounting crime and soical unrest.

THE THIRD TRUMPET

The sound from the third trumpet will signal a heavenly body, a star, to descend to the earth (see Revelation 8:10). The effect of this star hitting the ground will be to make one-third of the rivers and streams bitter and undrinkable. John found it easy to describe exactly what happened here, as he revealed that the name of the heavenly body will be Wormwood. Wormwood, or absinthe as we know it today, is a bitter, intoxicating, and poisonous herb. Too much of it can cause convulsions, paralysis, and death. So, now, coupled with the pangs of hunger, people will also be suffering from thirst. One-third of all the waters in the world will be polluted, bitter, and undrinkable.

THE FOURTH TRUMPET

The previous three trumpets will have brought down judgments wreaking havoc on land, trees, grass, seas, rivers, streams, springs, etc. However, with the blast from the fourth trumpet supernatural occurrences will take place in the heavens. All natural light will be diminished by one-third (see Revelation 8:12). The strength of the sun will be reduced by one-third.

The summer sun will appear pale and weak; the winter sun, watery and feeble. Because the moon draws its light from the sun, it, too, will inevitably be affected. The pull of gravity from the moon controls the tides. Who knows what effect this diminished power will have on the seas?

The stars will also be affected. One-third of the stars will be darkened. The dim moon and the darkened stars will make the night blacker than we have ever known it to be. What a cold, gloomy place the world will become!

Some Bible scholars have interpreted Revelation 8:12 to mean that the daylight will literally be shortened by one-third, resulting in the night being lengthened by one-third. That would mean an average of about sixteen hours of darkness every day! Anyway we look at it, it is certainly possible that God will extend the darkness of the night. However, whichever way it is interpreted, the end result will be the same—disruption of order followed by confusion, fear, and chaos.

Revelation 8:13 indicates that there will be a pause in the sequence of the trumpet judgments. A different angel will be heard crying, "Woe, woe, woe, to the inhabiters of the earth by reason of the other voices of the trumpet of the three angels, which are yet to sound!" The judgments will be intensifying. It seems as if God will be giving the inhabitants of earth one more warning of what will be coming upon them. They will still have a chance to repent.

THE FIFTH TRUMPET

Whereas the first four trumpet judgments will be directed against earth's ecology, the next three will be directed against man himself.

As he heard the fifth trumpet sound, John saw an angel descending to earth with a key in his hand. This key will open the door of the bottomless pit, where all kinds of evil beings have been imprisoned. With the handing over of the key God will be giving Satan authority to do as he wills. Now man wants the spirit world; in that day he will get it, and it will be so indescribably horrible that he will beg to die, but will not be able to.

As soon as the pit is opened, a thick blackness will belch from it. Out of this blackness will come living creatures, horrible in shape, mean and malevolent in disposition, and with the ability to inflict pain and suffering on man. John called them locusts, but they will not be locusts as we know them. These will be supernatural, infernal beings. Unlike earthly locusts, these locusts will be commanded not to "hurt the grass of the earth, neither any green thing, neither any tree; but only those men which have not the seal of God in their foreheads" (Revelation 9:4).

Their job will be to torment all those who do not have the seal of God in their foreheads. This indicates to us that they will possess some intelligence, as they will have to discriminate between those who have this seal and those who do not.

Revelation 9:5 says, "And their torment was as the torment of a scorpion, when he striketh a man." The pain inflicted by these demonized locusts of the Tribulation will be so intense that people will do anything they can to escape—even to attempt suicide. But verse 6 says, "Death shall flee from them." For the first time in man's existence, he will not have a choice over whether he lives or dies. No matter what he does, death will elude him. This dreadful torment will go on for a period of five months—though it will probably seem like five years!

THE SIXTH TRUMPET

At the sounding of the sixth trumpet the voice from the altar will command the four bound angels at the Euphrates River to be released. Whatever will have been holding them back will be removed, and they will be freed. At once we see the mobilization of a mighty army from the East. Motivated by Satan, 200 million persons pictured as demon horsemen, will rise up and begin marching toward the west to cross the Euphrates River.

Until this century no power in the world could possibly mobilize 200 million persons. However, this has now changed. Red China has the military personnel and potential military might to accomplish what John saw in his vision. Many Bible scholars believe that Revelation 9:16 is, in fact, referring to a giant confederacy of Oriental nations with Red China being the leader. On the other hand, this could well be a mighty demon force energized by the power of Satan and representing one of his last-ditch efforts to annihilate mankind.

At any rate, for thirteen months this colossal army will ravage its way across Asia destroying everything in its path. The devastating aftermath will be that one-third of the remaining population of the world will die. We might think, *Surely after this the world will turn to God for mercy, and He will halt His terrible judgment!* But Revelation 9:20, 21 tells us that this will not happen.

THE LITTLE BOOK

Before the sounding of the seventh trumpet there will be a short interlude.

As we read of this, our attention is turned back to the activities in heaven. John saw a mighty angel step down from heaven and place one foot on the sea and one foot on the earth. In his hand he carried a little book. The opening of it or breaking of its seals began the first judgments of God upon the earth. Now that it had been opened, John was told to take it and "eat it up" (Revelation 10:9). While it would taste good in his mouth, it would turn bitter in his stomach.

In this metaphor we see a picture of John's dilemma. He wanted God's program to move forward to the day when Christ would return to earth as King of kings; he rejoiced in Christ's coming triumph. But when he looked at what was yet to come upon the earth before this could be accomplished, he shuddered—the horror of it all was like a bitter taste to him.

Then we come to a story that is placed almost in parenthesis in the unfolding drama. John was told about two witnesses who will be God's evangelists on the earth during the Tribulation period. Fearlessly these two witnesses will denounce the world ruler and expose him for what he really is. In addition, God will give them supernatural powers as evidenced in their ability to turn water to blood, to delay rain, and to bring plagues on the earth. They will be like a conscience that will not be silenced. So the people will try to kill them, but for some mysterious reason they will not be successful. The length of the two witnesses' ministry has been planned by God, and only when it is ended, will they die. God will give them supernatural ability to avoid death until their time has been fulfilled.

When finally the forty-two months of their ministry are completed, the world ruler will seize them and kill them. The populace will be jubilant! People will be so glad to be rid of these two witnesses that they will give each other gifts in celebration. To teach the rest of the world a lesson, the Antichrist will leave the bodies of the two witnesses lying in the street for three and a half days for everyone to see. (Read Revelation 11:9.)

Then, the scene will change. The celebration and jubilation will come to a screeching halt at the end of three and a half days. After eighty-four hours of death the two witnesses will miraculously be brought back to life by God. While Christians who met Christ in the Rapture will have simply disappeared, the whole world will watch as these two faithful witnesses ascend to be with almighty God.

As if to emphasize what has taken place, a violent earthquake will shake the land. The remnant will be afraid and awe-stricken and will recognize this as coming from the God of heaven. However, this will be merely a recognition of fear; there will be no true repentance toward God.

THE SEVENTH TRUMPET

The seventh trumpet will not unleash immediate judgment on creation as the previous six will have done. Instead, it will cause great commotion in heaven as all the inhabitants will preview the program or outline of events still to come. They will see that there is to be a radical change in the government of the world when the world's kingdoms "become the kingdoms of our Lord" (Revelation 11:15). They will see the angry nations and watch their final destruction. They will see the resurrection of the wicked dead and their judgment, and they will see rewards given to the believers (Revelation 11:18). They will see these coming events culminate in the triumphant return of Christ to the earth.

Finally, chapter 11 closes with flashes of lightning and violent peals of thunder—a warning that God's final climactic judgments are still to fall on those who continue to reject His Son.

This theme of activity in heaven is continued into chapter 12. Several things appear on the scene:

First, John saw a woman about to give birth to a child. Standing near the woman was a red dragon waiting to pounce on the newborn child. However, when the male child was born, God snatched him up to heaven and safety. The woman then fled to a place of safety and remained there for about three and a half years.

The woman is symbolic of the nation of Israel; the male child represents the 144,000 Jews who will emerge from Israel and will be sealed of God. The dragon is a symbol of Satan, who, working through the Antichrist, will wait to destroy these 144,000 Jewish evangelists. However, before he will get a chance, God will catch them up to heaven. In retaliation Satan and the Antichrist will turn on the nation of Israel. At this time the Antichrist will break his covenant with Israel and will persecute the Jews unmercifully. These afflicted people then will flee into the wilderness of Edom and Moab (modern Jordan and Arabia) and hide there for the remainder of the Tribulation period.

Then war will break out in heaven. Satan's time of power and authority will be getting short, so not only will he lash out against Israel, but he and his army of fallen angels will invade heaven to try to wrest authority from God. Michael and his angels will battle with the forces of Satan and overcome them. They will be banished from heaven forever.

It sounds incredible, doesn't it? In reality, it is the truth of God bringing His world to a close. Seven trumpets will announce the judgment of God and challenge the world to repent. It will be a sad day, but for the Christian it will be a glad day.

The important thing for us is that "now is the day of salvation" (2 Corinthians 6:2). Our committment today determines our destiny tomorrow!

THE RISE OF
THE ANTICHRIST

*And I stood upon the sand of the sea, and saw
a beast rise up out of the sea, having seven heads
and ten horns, and upon his horns ten crowns, and
upon his heads the name of blasphemy. And the
beast which I saw was like unto a leopard, and his
feet were as the feet of a bear, and his mouth as the
mouth of a lion: and the dragon gave him his power,
and his seat, and great authority* (Revelation 13:1, 2).

Sounds like a scene from a science-fiction story,
doesn't it? And it gets worse! The narrative goes on
to say that this beast looked like a leopard with the
feet of a bear and the mouth of a lion and that its
power came from a dragon.

The description above is highly symbolic; but it is
important for us to realize that it isn't fiction, even
though it may sound like it. What this all refers to
is the rise of a single man—the beast—who will be
king of one nation and will eventually rule over a
worldwide confederacy of ten nations. The phrase
"feet of a bear" suggests huge armies mighty enough
to crush rebellions. The phrase "mouth of a lion"
refers to great power. The beast will have the body
of a leopard, which symbolizes agility and swiftness.
The dragon, which will give the beast its power, is

73

Satan. Thus, both the man who is the Antichrist and the empire he rules will be wicked beyond measure, and they will be in direct opposition to everything which pertains to God.

There is much to be said about the man Antichrist, but it is first necessary to see how the world is being prepared for his coming. History does not move along in isolated events. It moves along in a growth process—one event merging into another—one event preparing the way for another. Thus, we see that the world has to be prepared emotionally, mentally, and psychologically for the person of the Antichrist. The spirit of Antichrist is already prevalent in the world. We have seen strange and subversive forces invade our governmental agencies, their influence reaching all the way to the White House. In the world today there is more dread, anxiety, and fear than ever before in our history. Alcoholism and teenage suicide have soared. Almost one million children are now receiving some kind of psychiatric care, and incidents of child abuse have grown so sharply that in one issue of a metropolitan newspaper there were two articles dealing with proposed measures to alleviate this problem. U. S. physicians have reported that they now treat some 1.5 million cases of child abuse every year. Out of this total, fifty thousand children are killed each year (137 daily) in beatings.

In his recent book *Whatever Became of Sin,* Karl Menninger states: "There is a constant cloud of gloom and dread that seems to have settled all over the world." Another psychologist suggests that the world is suffering from a massive nervous breakdown.

As we search God's Word for references to this spirit of Antichrist, we hear John say, "Little children, it is the last time: and as ye have heard that antichrist shall come, even now are there many antichrists; whereby we know that it is the last time" (1 John 2:18). In verse 22 he continued, "Who is a liar but he that denieth that Jesus is the Christ? He is antichrist, that denieth the Father and the Son." Again, in 2 John 1:7, he wrote, "For many deceivers are entered into the world, who confess not that Jesus Christ is come in the flesh. This is a deceiver and an antichrist."

This spirit of Antichrist, then, is an unseen force that will work on the mind or psychology of the people. No one will escape it—no one will be exempt. It will bring with it false christs, crumbling family relationships, and lawlessness; and these will be seen in a greater degree than ever before. We see that the spirit of Antichrist has been in the world since early in the history of the church— that it is growing and spreading and will ultimately culminate in the person of one man.

Well, then, what about the person of the Antichrist? When will he come? How will he rise to power? What will he be like?

WHEN WILL HE COME?

Jesus tells us that the days will be as the days of Noah, "for as in the days that were before the flood they were eating and drinking, marrying and giving in marriage, until the day that Noe entered into the ark" (Matthew 24:38). This was a time of great prosperity; civilization was at a peak. We see a definite parallel here, because the same kind of climate exists in our world today.

It is likely that the appearance of the Antichrist on the scene will be rather sudden. In the book of Daniel the vision shows a "little horn" that comes up among ten horns of the beast (see Daniel 7:8). The ten horns signify the ten powerful kings of a large confederacy. Apparently, the Antichrist will make his appearance as a rather obscure king or leader of another smaller nation. Therefore, we know that these ten kingdoms must be established before we can look for the revealing of the Antichrist. It is likely we will begin to see the emergence of these kingdoms sometime before the Rapture. While we believe the Rapture will take the Church out of the world before the Tribulation begins, there is little doubt we will have a foretaste of the Tribulation to come. In his book *What in the World Will Happen Next?* Salem Kirban makes the following observations:

> *The oil shortage already affects thousands of household products.*
>
> *Many families now find their breadwinner out of a job because of the energy shortage.*
>
> *Thermostats must be set at 68⁰ to assure fuel for the winters.*
>
> *In the twenty-year period from 1952 to 1972 food costs zoomed up 62 percent; home ownership costs, 91.7 percent.*
>
> *To escape from reality, Americans spent $100 billion in one year on leisure alone.*

Schools have found it impossible to enforce dress standards. School property destruction caused by students has now reached epidemic proportions. In five years vandalism in New York City schools rose from $2 million to $4 million!

Witchcraft, black magic, and Satanism are now popular subjects in many colleges.

Suicides among high school students are on the increase.

Famine is raging across the world with Africa experiencing its most severe drought in sixty years. Millions have died.

UFO sightings have reached an unprecedented high.

Courses on mysticism covering witchcraft and the holding of seances are being taught in high schools.

The Satan cult is spreading rapidly with ritualistic murders and suicides.

(Salem Kirban, *What in the World Will Happen Next?* pp. 21, 29, 31, 43.)

From these observations and the front pages of our own newspapers, we can clearly see that the spirit of Antichrist pervades our world today and is rapidly affecting the life-style of each and every one of us.

HOW WILL HE RISE TO POWER?

In a miraculous way this obscure king will overthrow the other kingdoms in the confederacy and gain control of the federation of ten nations. With the supernatural powers given to him by Satan he will astonish the world and gradually take control of forces that will ultimately lead to complete world domination. This powerful leader will unite the ten nations, bringing order out of chaos, and emerge as a great peacemaker and humanitarian.

WHAT WILL HE BE LIKE?

Satan himself can be transformed into an "angel of light" (2 Corinthians 11:14), and he will bestow upon this man such attributes as charm, wit, and intelligence so that he will deceive many. The Antichrist will be a dynamic speaker, self-assured, and proud. As he establishes himself as a savior of the world, he will take special pains to become a friend of the Jews. Besides being a brilliant diplomat, he will be a superb strategist. He may offer Israel unlimited military aid; such as, jet planes and nuclear missiles. He will appear to be an answer to prayer and will undoubtedly persuade Israel that he has come to protect them and usher in the Golden Age—the Messianic Age—for the Jewish race. Israel will flourish and prosper, and world economy will be at an all-time high. For three and one-half years he will reign supreme.

THEN WHAT?

After three and one-half years this man's true nature will be revealed. His treaty with Israel will be broken, and he will move from a tactic of peace to one of crushing power. He will declare himself a world dictator and will move to eliminate all opposition. Following this will be three and one-half years of horror. These forty-two months will be the period Jesus spoke of when He described "great tribulation, such as was not since the beginning of the world to this time, no, nor ever shall be" (Matthew 24:21). The Antichrist will be given power and authority to make war on the saints. The Temple will be defiled and cursing and blasphemies will fill the air. (Read Revelation 13:4-7.)

At this point a new character will be introduced into the scene. (Read Revelation 13:11-17.)

The second beast spoken of by John completes the "Unholy Trinity": Satan, the Antichrist, and the False Prophet. This False Prophet will be the antithesis of the Holy Spirit, just as the Antichrist will be a counterfeit of Jesus Christ. The False Prophet will have great power and will do great wonders. Because of these great wonders he will deceive many and become very powerful. Rather than call attention to himself, he will function to exalt, to edify, and to cause the people of the earth to worship the Antichrist. He will erect images of him everywhere, and will even have the power to cause these images to speak. These images could be giant computers or automated dolls. We've all heard ventriloquists "throw" their voice into a doll or a stuffed animal. This is a commonly used theatrical trick. But since we are speaking here of a society that will be technically well-advanced, these speaking images will have to be a more sophisticated deception. We do know that all the powers of the False Prophet will be either clever imitations or the actual supernatural work of the devil himself.

It is the False Prophet who will institute the mark of the beast. Loyalty to the beast will have to be openly affirmed. He will devise a system of marking to separate the true followers of the beast from the followers of Christ. The pressure will be

79

on! If a person does not take the mark, he will not be able to buy, sell, or receive any medical care or any kind of services whatever. He will be subject to persecution and death.

In this way God will allow the first beast, the Antichrist, to achieve a universal dominion, and multitudes will follow him. Satan will enjoy a temporary victory.

Well, what specifically will this Antichrist do? How will he go about maintaining control of the world? Three books of the Bible tell us:

1. He will change times and laws (Daniel 7:25).
2. He will understand mysteries and solve problems (Daniel 8:23).
3. He will work signs and wonders (Daniel 8:24).
4. He will cause prosperity and peace (Daniel 8:25).
5. He will persecute and destroy Israel (Daniel 9:24-27).
6. He will control money and riches (Daniel 11:43).
7. He will control religion and worship (2 Thessalonians 2:4).
8. He will perform lying signs and wonders (2 Thessalonians 2:9).
9. He will cause great deception (2 Thessalonians 2:11).
10. He will kill the two witnesses (Revelation 11:7).
11. He will reign supreme (Revelation 13:4).
12. He will blaspheme God (Revelation 13:6).

13. He will make war with and overcome the saints (Revelation 13:7).
14. He will exert power over the entire world (Revelation 13:7).
15. He will receive worship from the world (Revelation 13:8).

As we look back over the long list of acts attributed to this Antichrist, it isn't difficult to see that the beginnings of these things are already evident. The recent revival of interest in the occult, psychic phenomena, and Satan worship; the development of drug therapy aimed at mood alteration and behavior modification; and the increased use of computerized accounts in the financial world are but a few reminders of how easily one man could take control of the entire world.

It is obvious that the foundation is being laid for the advent of a dictator. Concerned people are saying that the problems and tensions of the world need to be controlled by a strong hand. Arnold Toynbee, an eminent historian, commented on a radio broadcast that mankind has been brought to such a "degree of distress that we are ripe for the deifying of any new Caesar who might succeed in giving the world unity and peace."

The stage is set—it could be that the actors are all in their places awaiting their cues to begin the final act in the history of mankind on earth.

8

SEVEN
LAST PLAGUES

Plague!

The word itself strikes terror into the hearts of people whose country frequently becomes ridden with infectious diseases. We read of the "Black Death" in the fourteenth century when 25 million persons—nearly one fourth of the population of Europe—died in the epidemic.

All through the Bible we read of the plagues or calamities sent by God as punishment. In Genesis 12:17, we read, the Lord sent a plague upon the house of Pharaoh because he had taken Sarai, Abram's wife. In Exodus 7:20 through 12:36 the story is told of how God sent ten plagues upon Egypt because the Pharaoh would not release His people. In Leviticus 26:21 God warned Israel that He would send seven times more plagues upon them according to their sins. Again in Jeremiah 19:8 He promised to punish Israel by plagues for her evil ways. Down through history, we see, plagues have been used extensively by God. The future will be no exception.

We have read of the seven trumpets, and we have seen through the eyes of John the wrath of God as it will begin to be poured out on humanity. As the pace of the book of Revelation increases, we find the day of patience and mercy rapidly coming to an end.

No more the sacrificial Lamb of God, but King of kings and Lord of Lords, we see Jesus ready to bring judgment with a "sharp sickle"—swift and terrifying. (Read Revelation 14:14.)

"Filled up" and overflowing, the most appalling judgments ever dreamed of will be unleashed as seven angels pour out God's wrath from seven different bowls or vials. (Read Revelation 15:1.)

FIRST VIAL

(Painful Sores; Revelation 16:2)

It is interesting to notice that these "noisome and grievous" sores will occur only among those who have taken the mark of the beast. Perhaps this mark will involve something similar to the modern tattoo, which could become infected. Or perhaps these sores will in some way be connected to the ulcerated sore that accompanies venereal disease. Assuredly the permissive attitude already permeating our society toward loose moral standards could lead in that direction. But whatever the nature and cause, we know these sores will be painful and unsightly—a true judgment on those who reject the healing power of the Great Physician.

SECOND AND THIRD VIALS

(Death in Seas; Rivers and Waters Turn to Blood) (Revelation 16:3, 4)

The Amplified Bible tells us that these waters will not be just the color of blood but "like that of a corpse [thick, corrupt, ill-smelling, and disgusting]." We know from Exodus 7:20-25 that God once before resorted to this rather drastic action when He turned the waters of the Nile into blood. When we attempt to look at this phenomenon in the light of our own experience, we find the idea not too far-fetched.

In her best-selling novel, *Silent Spring,* Rachel Carson reported that in June, 1954, planes carrying loads of pesticides flew over the forests on the banks of the Miramichi River on the coast of New Brunswick. The project was designed to save the forests from the spruce budworm, but within two days of the spraying hundreds of dead and dying fish were found along the banks of the river. (Rachel Carson, *Silent Spring,* 1962, p. 131.) With the war against the insect world that is being waged in ever-increasing intensity, it isn't difficult to imagine that we could eventually find our seas and rivers actually "turned to blood" from the bursting bodies of the fish that become the hapless victims of eradication efforts. Thus, we see not only the loss of the drinking supply but of a major portion of the food supply as well.

FOURTH VIAL

(Sun Scorches All Mankind; Revelation 16:8, 9)

From ages past men have worshiped the sun. Today scientists acclaim its life-sustaining power. In the long summer months even we know that the unrelenting rays of the sun beating down on a concrete pavement can produce enough heat literally to "fry an egg." In this fourth vial judgment of God, we see, the sun will no longer be a benefactor of man but a persecutor. There will be no escape. We don't know if this judgment will be caused by some cataclysmic upheaval that might

85

blast the earth out of its natural orbit and bring it closer to the sun, or if God's supernatural power will be brought to bear to increase the power of the sun. It really isn't important. What is important is that rather than turn to God for mercy, acknowledging that their own sinful natures have caused all these disasters, men will blaspheme His name, cursing Him for bringing such evils upon them.

FIFTH VIAL

(Darkness; Revelation 16:10, 11)

It appears that these seven vials of wrath will be poured out in quick success. If so, a mass of humanity will be writhing under a scorching heat one day and the next day will be plunged into total darkness. The area affected by this particular judgment will be the throne and the kingdom of the Antichrist, or the territory encompassed by the old Roman Empire. Apparently only the followers of Antichrist will be consumed with such pain that they will go into convulsions.

Again, let us try to see this situation in contemporary times. It is not too fantastic to imagine that extreme temperatures generated from the scorching rays of the sun the day before could cause a massive power failure, due to overloaded air-conditioning equipment. In addition, smog generated by modern factories could cause the sun to be darkened and the moon not to shed its light, in direct fulfillment of Matthew 24:29. In any event, it isn't difficult to picture the chaos that will result. What disorientation! What panic! But still men will not repent of their deeds.

SIXTH VIAL

(River Euphrates Dries Up; Revelation 16:12)

Here, we see preparation being made for the Battle of Armageddon. We have already noted in our study this quarter that when the sixth trumpet is sounded, an army of 200 million horsemen will begin their march to slay one-third of the men on earth. It seems that the pouring out of the vials of wrath will be similar in nature, but greater in scope, than the seven trumpet judgments. Thus, we can expect that the "kings of the east" with their armies will involve great multitudes.

The Euphrates River is a great and renowned stream, which has cradled such early civilizations as the Babylonians and Assyrians. It winds some 1,700 miles flowing southeast into the Persian Gulf. If you examine this area on a globe, you will see its strategic position. Africa, Palestine, and Arabia are to the southwest; Russia, China, India, and Iran are to the northeast. The Euphrates is the dividing line. Thus, if a great land army composed of forces from the East—possibly some combination of Russia, China, India, Iran, and Japan —desired to invade Palestine, this river would be a formidable barrier.

In the Scripture, however, we see that this great river will be dried up so the "kings of the east" may cross over. They will be assisted on their way to their final destruction. (Read Revelation 16:13, 14.)

Before we examine the final vial we are shown that these vials will lead up to the final showdown Battle of Armageddon. Unclean spirits will go abroad in the world inciting the kings of the earth to make war on Israel.

SEVENTH VIAL

(A Great Earthquake; Revelation 16:16-20)

Are not the words "It is done!" faintly reminiscent of another time? As we think back, we are reminded that then, too, thunders, darkened skies, and earthquakes shook the earth. And we recall a voice in dying agony whispering, "It is finished!" (See John 19:30; Matthew 27:45-54.)

God says, "Vengeance is mine; I will repay" (Romans 12:19), and repay He does! After centuries of patience and mercy, God will at last execute final judgment on those who have scorned, ridiculed, and rejected His Son. All the elements of nature will be shaken as the seventh angel pours out his vial into the air.

As the armies from the East clash with the forces of Israel on this historic battleground— where Saul died in a battle with the Philistines (1 Samuel 31:1) and Josiah was slain in a battle with Pharaoh-nechoh (2 Kings 23:29, 30)—the earth will stagger and reel under the force of the most violent earthquake ever known to man. Thunder and lightnings will rend the skies. Mountains will crumble. Islands will sink into the sea. The foundations of cities throughout the world will be shaken. Buildings will come toppling down. People will run frantically for safety. But all will be in vain, as the wrath of God is released in a final, cataclysmic upheaval.

It is apparent that these seven vials of God's wrath *can* be of supernatural origin. We know from the Scriptures that God in His displeasure has caused plagues, rivers of blood, earthquakes, rain of fire and hail, and the like to fall on mankind.

It is interesting to note, however, that all the calamities depicted in these seven vials of wrath can conceivably be caused by man himself. God in His infinite goodness and wisdom created for man an earth of unparalleled beauty: with clear blue skies, streams, lakes sparkling like crystal in the sunlight, trees, shrubbery, and flowers delicately scented and of unimaginable variety. Man has been given a virtual paradise, but man has been careless with his inheritance. He has littered the landscape with throw-away bottles, plates, and cups; he has dumped polluting wastes into his once clear streams; he has poured noxious fumes into the sky from belching smokestacks; he has done all this in the name of progress.

God created a world in delicate balance. Man has upset that balance. In an attempt to control hurricanes he has developed methods of "seeding" potential hurricane clouds. Now scientists are beginning to see that hurricanes serve a definite purpose in keeping heat and energy levels in balance. In an attempt to control insect infestation, man has also seriously endangered the fish and bird population of the earth. We are just now beginning to suspect that God knew what He was doing after all.

This is not to say that God's plans for the ultimate destruction of this earth would or could be diverted by a change in our treatment of the lovely planet He gave us. The issue is not that simple. We have sinned against God. We have rejected His Son. We have disobeyed God's Word. And we can be assured that, as a result, we have brought on ourselves the judgment of the seven vials of wrath.

9

DATELINE
BABYLON

Bible Reading:

Revelation 17:1-5, 15-18
18:1-3, 8-10, 15-19

Ancient Babylon? in the middle of the book of Revelation? How in the world does this fit in and what significance could be attached to a city that no longer even exists?

Well, nothing is placed in the Holy Scriptures by chance; everything has a purpose and meaning. Perhaps as we look a little closer at Revelation 17 and 18, we'll discover what God was saying as He revealed His plan to John.

These two chapters give an overview of the state of things on earth after the rapture of the Church and during the Tribulation period. They are parenthetically inserted to give us a clearer picture of the events leading up to the outpouring of God's judgments and the conditions that will prevail at that time.

Two Babylons are actually referred to in Revelation 17 and 18. Chapter 17 deals with the religious system symbolized by that ancient city; and chapter 18 concerns itself with the people, attitudes, and importance of the city itself. Both the system and the city will be the recipients of God's condemnation.

BABYLON: A RELIGIOUS SYSTEM

Nimrod was a rebel. The great-grandson of Noah, Nimrod had been taught from his earliest years what God expected of him and how he was to live. He had heard the story many, many times of how God destroyed the world by flood. He also knew why God did this: to wipe out the evil and corruption of the people on earth.

But Nimrod got tired of doing things God's way and decided to branch out on his own. He gathered together a group of people and talked them into moving to a new area and starting a new community. They would settle in the flat, fertile plain of Shinar on the banks of the Euphrates River. There they would establish their own way of life and worship in the way they chose.

Nimrod was an ambitious man. Once he got his group settled in the land of Shinar, they immediately got busy building a city; and Genesis 11:3 says, "They had brick for stone, and slime had they for morter." This was the start of the brickmaking industry. The slime of this area was so tenacious that even today archaeologists find it is almost impossible to detach things cemented with it.

But one thing bugged Nimrod. He was afraid that all his followers would scatter in time and that he would lose the dictatorial power he held over them. So he came up with the idea of building an enormous tower. This would be the means by which they would find out everything they wanted to know about the heavens and the gods. With the stars to guide them and idols to worship, they wouldn't need a God whom they couldn't see, hear, or touch. Nimrod therefore declared his open rebellion to God. God had said: "Be fruitful, and multiply, and replenish the earth" (Genesis 9:1), indicating that man should scatter into all areas. But Nimrod said, "Let's all stay right here and do our own thing." So they began work on the construction of the tower.

A description of this tower discovered in 1876 tells us that there were seven sections, each twenty feet high and each decreasing in width to the top. Around the base were shrines to various gods, and on the top platform was a sanctuary for the god Bel-Merodach displaying the signs of the Zodiac. (Astrology is certainly nothing new!)

When God saw the activities of Nimrod and his friends, He was displeased. As punishment God caused them to speak different languages. The result? Mass confusion. One day a man's neighbor spoke the same language he did; the next day he couldn't understand his neighbor and his neighbor couldn't understand him! So they called the tower Babel, meaning "confusion."

Up to this time the whole race had had one language, and all idolatrous worshipers had had one form of religion. But when God confounded their language, men began to disagree on religion and other matters. This caused them to branch out into sects, where each one did things the way he thought best. In the end men did scatter, just as God had intended they should.

But the damage had already been done. Nimrod had introduced the people to an anti-God way of life. He had ushered in a system of religion that was to be the birthplace of all the false teachings that were to creep in throughout history. He had formed the seedbed of all the things that Satan would afterward introduce into the world of religion thus, we see the beginning of the city they called "Babylon."

Many centuries passed and the Babylonian cult spread and grew in acceptance and popularity. The objects of worship were the Supreme Father, the Incarnate Female or Queen of Heaven, and Her Son. The cult claimed to have the most divine secrets and the highest wisdom, and many mysterious rites were performed. It was here that confession to priests was introduced. By the time Nebuchadnezzar came to rule over the Babylonian Empire, this cult was the accepted religion of the people. Here we see the monarchy assuming dictatorial powers by commanding the people: "Worship the image I have erected, or die!"

The Babylonian Empire crumbled in time, and the Roman Empire emerged as a great power in the world. In 63 B.C. Julius Caesar became the head of the Roman branch of the Babylonian cult. From then on, whoever ruled the Roman Empire also ruled the religious system of priestcraft, idolatry, devil worship, and all the many other things that went along with it.

Around 313 A.D. Constantine became emperor of Rome. He succeeded Diocletian who had persecuted the Christians unmercifully. Constantine is reputed to have been a friend of the early Christians, but on closer investigation we learn that he was also an astute politician. He wanted control of the whole world, and standing in his way was the Christian church. His predecessor had tried persecuting the Christians, but that had only caused Christianity to spread.

Constantine decided on a different approach. He reversed the order. He went all out to win the favor of the Christians. He allocated certain of the heathen temples and palaces for Christian worship: he introduced vestments for the bishops; he even acted as moderator at the council of Nicea where all the leaders of the early Christian church had gathered.

History tells us that in one year over twelve thousand converts to Christianity were given a white robe and twenty pieces of gold each to get them into the church. Slowly but surely politics was creeping into the Christian church. This period marked the beginning of the union of church and state.

When Demasus, a bishop of the Christian church at Rome, was elected to its headship in A.D. 366 Babylonianism and organized Christianity became one. The rites of Babylon were soon introduced into the Christian church. Worship and veneration of images and relics, private confessions to priests, penances and scourgings, which had originated with pagan rites and festivals, little by little became a part of Christian worship.

Satan could not destroy the church of Jesus Christ through persecution and martyrdom; so he subtly set about diminishing its effectiveness by diverting its attention to the forms and ceremonies practiced by the pagans. This diluted form of Christianity would be much more popular with the masses, and many more people would accept the Christian way of worship. The result was that the people were deceived into believing a religion that down through the ages has done more damage to the church of Jesus Christ than outright persecution could have done. It was a master stroke for Satan.

So now we can see the pattern. Nimrod's rebellion turned people away from God to idolatry and witchcraft. These idolatrous practices subsequently became the religion of the rulers, who in turn made them the religion of the people. Through a purely political move, the new Christian church was wooed into trusting a seemingly sympathetic emperor. This emperor won their favor by handing over to them former heathen temples in which to worship. The transition was completed when Demasus incorporated heathen forms of worship into Christian services.

Out of this merger have sprung all the religions and religious practices we find in the world today. They cover the full spectrum of religious worship —from idolatrous heathenism to religions so closely approximating true Christianity that you have to look closely to identify them as being false. This is precisely why ancient Babylon is referred to in the book of Revelation.

A woman is often used as a symbol in Scripture. The church of Jesus Christ, incorporating all true believers of every age, is referred to as the "bride" of Christ—pure and faithful. The woman described by John in Revelation 17 is the exact opposite—a prostitute and unfaithful. This woman represents the false religious system that originated with Nimrod. This false, religious system was unfaithful to the God it claimed to love and aligned itself with those who hated the true God. Verse 2 tells us, "It is with her that the kings of the earth have debauched themselves and the inhabitants of the earth have become drunk on the wine of her filthiness" (*Phillips*).

All the nations of the earth have been affected

by this false religious system. Around two-thirds of the world population today are pagan idolaters; the majority of the other third is made up of Muslims, Catholics, Jews, infidels, or adherents of some questionable and antichristian faith and worship.

This false religious system has tremendous influence and vast wealth. Revelation 17:15 says, "The waters which thou sawest, where the whore sitteth, are peoples, and multitudes, and nations, and tongues." It appears that every kingdom or government on earth today embodies and exhibits the spirit and rebellion of Nimrod. Few, if any, accept the spirit and commandments of God. The nations and peoples have been seduced away from the true God. The woman is also "arrayed in purple and scarlet colour, and decked with gold and precious stones and pearls, having a golden cup in her hand" (Revelation 17:4).

As John looked at this woman, he saw that she was "drunken with the blood of the saints, and with the blood of the martyrs of Jesus" (Revelation 17:6). Babylonianism has a history soaked in blood. Since its inception those who have chosen to stand against its practices and teachings have paid with their lives. How many of the faithful have been branded as heretics and paid for their religious convictions by being stretched on a rack, burned at the stake, tortured, and killed? And all this has been done not to appease some heathen deity but in the name of so-called civilized Christianity! Even today Christians behind the Iron Curtain are being imprisoned, tortured, and killed for their faith.

This woman is seen riding on a strange-looking beast with seven heads and ten horns. The beast referred to here is the same as the one in chapter 13—the Antichrist. The seven heads represent the seven empires that will have coexisted with Israel from her beginning: (1) Egyptian, (2) Assyrian, (3) Babylonian, (4) Medo-Persian, (5) Greek, (6) Roman, and (7) Revised Roman, under the rule of the Antichrist. The ten horns are the ten rulers who will rise up with the Antichrist and support him in his reign.

The woman's riding on the beast indicates an alliance and cooperation between the beast (Antichrist) and the woman (religious system). How could this ever come about? For several years now religious leaders have indicated their desire to break down the barriers that divide them and to promote better understanding between differing religious faiths. The World Council of Churches has been formed to explore common areas of doctrine and belief. While it is doing this, however, it also is playing an increasingly important political role, particularly in regard to what is known as the Third World nations. These are the developing nations of the world, consisting of major portions of the Pacific islands, the Middle East, the Far East, Africa, Central America, and South America. Pope Paul VI recently intimated that he believed the Roman Catholic Church would figure more prominently in the affairs of this World Council in the future. For one reason or another the institutionalized church is banding together to form a world church system.

The church has always wanted power and has prostituted herself again and again to try to attain that power. With the arrival of the Antichrist on

98

the scene, the church will see an excellent chance to achieve the domination and control she craves. What better way to solve the world's problems than with the leadership of the Antichrist and the humanism of the church? For his part, the Antichrist will see in the church a powerful force to be wooed and won before he can gain absolute control of humanity. Also, the wealth of the church will seem a prize worth catching! So the Antichrist will seemingly go along with the organized church and use her to his own ends.

Finally the clash will come! There will be a gigantic conflict between the Antichrist's political kingdom and the apostate (renegade) church. We are not told what will bring about this division, but possibly the reason will be a struggle for power. The church will gain too much power, and the Antichrist will feel that the church is a growing threat to his sovereignty.

After wooing and winning the church, he will suddenly turn and lash out at her. So great will be his hatred that he will go all out to annihilate the church. The false religious system inspired by Satan and typified by Babylon will finally be destroyed by him. For the remainder of the Tribulation period there will be no open religious worship whatsoever. Those who turn to God during all the judgments will automatically be killed.

BABYLON: A CITY

Now we come to a different Babylon. The one referred to in chapter 18 is a city. Of all the famous cities of the ancient empires, there must have been something unusual about Babylon, for it to have been brought to our attention again in the book of Revelation. Let's take a closer look at what this city represents.

Babylon became the controlling seat of the great Babylonian Empire built by Nebuchadnezzar. When he came into power, he began invading the surrounding countries, capturing the inhabitants and carrying them back as his prisoners to Babylon. He spent the resources of his empire and the immense spoils of the conquered nations in the enlargement, embellishment, and fortification of his favorite city.

The Babylon he built or extended from the original was quite fabulous in its day—modern, scientifically designed, and quite impregnable. It was built in the form of an exact square covering 200 square miles of territory, with a surrounding inner wall and outer wall. Each section of the inner wall measured 15 miles in length, 87 feet in width, and 350 feet in height. The outer wall gave added protection to the city. Right through the middle ran the Euphrates River, splitting it equally into two parts.

The only means of access into the city was through the gates of the outer wall over the Euphrates River. Twenty-five solid brass gates in each inner wall gave entrance to the city itself. A road led directly from each gate across the city to the gate on the opposite side. If we could have seen it from the air, it would have looked like a neat checkerboard with giant squares (of 576 square feet) between roads.

In the center of the city were two palaces, one on either side of the river. These palaces were connected by a tunnel that ran under the river, thus providing a way of escape for the rulers in case of attack or supplying necessary food or communication in case of a seige.

One of Nebuchadnezzar's favorite wives was a woman who grew up in the highlands of Persia surrounded by mountains, trees, and shrubs. When she married and moved to Babylon, she could not adjust to the flatness of the countryside and longed for the beauty of her homeland.

Her indulgent husband decided to do something about this. Using beams, bricks, pipes, soil, and mortar, he constructed a replica of the area in which she grew up. He raised the land to form hills; he planted tall trees; he devised an irrigation system that drew water up from the river to water the shrubs and plants he had placed everywhere.

"Big deal!" you say? "So some guy with plenty of money and nothing to do between wars decided to build his wife a garden."

But wait a minute! This was about 600 B.C. The ingenuity, architectural planning, design, and construction required for such a feat in those days would be like trying to construct the Grand Canyon in the middle of the prairie today. It's no wonder Babylon came to be known as one of the Seven Wonders of the Ancient World! Its splendid towers and palaces and the pride and luxury of its inhabitants were proverbial among surrounding nations.

But one night, in spite of their smug assertion that the city was impregnable, Babylon was invaded. Cyrus and Darius, leaders of the Medes and Persians, hit on a brilliant strategy to conquer this city and all its wealth.

They learned that the Babylonians were to celebrate a great feast for several days, and as always during their great feasts, they would most likely be drunk most of the time and the city would not be closely guarded. Cyrus sent a party of his men to cut a channel into the banks of the Euphrates River and to divert the flow of water around the city wall. He then stationed half his men at one end of the city and half at the other.

When the flow of the Euphrates subsided to the point where they could wade through it, they marched under the outer city gates, through the opened, unguarded inner city gates, and right up to the palace. They surprised and slew the drunken king and his guards, and Darius took control of the kingdom. History tells us that because of the layout of Babylon, it was several hours before the other half of the city even realized that they had been invaded and conquered.

From that time on, Babylon's power and glory began to diminish. Before, man had gloried and boasted in his own achievements, strengths, military power, and might and had completely ignored almighty God. But God passed judgment on the city by the writing on the wall at Belshazzar's feast (Daniel 5:5) and performed what He said He would do.

Well, how does this ancient city tie in with what John was told in Revelation 18? There's no city of Babylon existing today. However, Zechariah said, in his prophecy, that Babylon would be rebuilt on the site of the ancient city, which is presently located about fifty-five miles south of Baghdad in the country of Iraq (Zechariah 5:11). It's possible that a city could be rebuilt on this ancient site; but is it possible that this city could become the center of wealth, influence, and commerce that Revelation 18 is referring to?

Well, where is the world's attention focused these days? The Middle East. Since the Arab oil embargo and the increase in the price of oil, billions of dollars have been pouring into these once poor countries. In 1975 Saudi Arabia, Iran, Iraq, Kuwait, the United Arab Emirates, and Qatar received $90 billion from oil sales. In contrast, Mideast oil revenues were only $15 billion in 1973.

What are they doing with all this newfound wealth? Some of it is being invested abroad, but most of it is being spent at home. Says James Conn, a vice-president of Bateman Eichler, Hill Richards, a California securities broker, "Many of these countries have been poor for a long time, and the first investment a poor person makes when he becomes wealthy is in himself." In an article, "Pursuing the Petrodollar," Art Detman says:

> Saudi Arabia, Iran and Iraq want to build industrial infrastructures. Plans call for new highways, railways, airports, power plants, cement plants, steel and aluminum mills, car and truck factories, desalinization plants, port facilities, oil refineries, chemical complexes, hospitals, telecommunications networks, housing units and even new cities. (Sky, *Delta Air Lines*, Vol. 4, Number 1, November, 1975.)

Certainly the potential is there for reconstruction of the ancient city of Babylon, even to the point of it becoming the center of world commerce. "Doing business in the Mideast is the greatest opportunity around right now," says Conn, of Bateman Eichler. "They're ready to buy if you have the right product—and price is not a material factor."

Major U. S. companies—like Lockheed Aircraft, Whittaker, General Motors, Fluor, General Telephone, and Rockwell—are investing in this area. U.S. hotel companies are planning new facilities. First National City Bank reopened its Cairo branch after twelve years and is adding new branches.

The soil in the area of old Babylon is exceedingly fertile, and engineers estimate that the Euphrates and Tigris rivers could irrigate seven million acres in winter and three million in summer to grow varied crops. Couple this flat, fertile plain with the unlimited money to develop it, and it becomes quite easy to imagine a thriving, modern, commercial center situated there.

But like Babylon of old, this new Babylon will incur the judgment of God. Why? Because they will again turn from God to worship other gods. This time, though, Babylon will concentrate its worship on the ephah and the talent (biblical symbols for commerce and industry). Such a worship will make temples out of banks, warehouses, exchanges, and pleasure parks. Such a worship will not pay homage to the sun, or moon, or stars, or emperors, or popes, but to dollars, pounds, francs and piasters. Such a worship, of greed and sensuous luxury, will be the worship of mammon (money) perfected and overriding and supplanting all other devotions.

Chapter 18 concludes by describing the judgment that will come upon new Babylon: sudden destruction by fire. One commentator remarks that beneath the area of old Babylon is a type of combustible asphalt. If it were to be hit by an earthquake, the city would easily be plunged into a devastating lake of fire.

As the city burns, three worlds made rich by

Babylon will stand far off and bewail their loss. First will be the *governmental world,* composed of the rulers and kings who enjoyed unprecedented power under Babylonian rule. Second will be the *commercial world,* which saturated itself with luxury and opulence through the opportunities of Babylon. Third will be the *maritime world,* whose ships plied between Babylon and the rest of the world. Together they will cry: "Alas, alas, that great city Babylon!" The city that exalted itself, shut out God, prided itself on its own achievements, pursued only wealth and material gain, and resorted to any means to attain its sinful goals will be no more!

The destruction of Babylon will cause great consternation on earth, but great rejoicing in heaven. All the hosts of heaven will unite in a voice of exultant adoration, saying, "Alleluia." They will praise God for judging the Great Harlot religious system that corrupted the earth, and they will praise Him for avenging the blood of His saints. The twenty-four elders and the four living creatures will also join in this chorus as the heavenly hosts worship God together.

Then we read that John heard a voice of a great multitude, like the sound of roaring and rushing waters or mighty thunderings, as the whole of heaven shouted, "Alleluia! For the Lord our God, the Almighty, has come into his kingdom!" (Revelation 19:6; *Phillips*). The hour of God's triumph will have come.

10

THE DIVINE INTERVENTION

Bible Reading:

Revelation 19:7-9, 11, 14, 15
19-21; 20:1-5

THE MARRIAGE

Did you know that there is going to be a wedding in heaven? So far we've learned of many things that will go on in heaven, but who would have thought that anything so "earthly" as a wedding would take place there? To get an idea of what this heavenly marriage is all about, let's examine the marriage customs of the period in which John lived.

Basically, three steps were involved leading to the actual ceremony. First, a marriage contract was negotiated between the parents, usually when the children were young. This contract was a binding agreement and meant that the pair were in actual fact legally married to each other, although they would have no sexual contact for years. This was known as a "betrothal," but it was a much stronger tie than our American "engagement." It gave the young couple a chance to grow in their relationship before taking their marriage vows.

The second step took place when the betrothed couple reached a suitable age of maturity. The groom, accompanied by his friends, would go to the bride's home and escort her to the new home that he had prepared for the two of them to live in.

Finally would come the consummating event, the wedding feast. Many guests would be invited to share the happiness of the bride and groom on this joyous occasion. (Adapted from *There's a New World Coming*, Hal Lindsey, p. 254.)

This beautiful picture of the union of a man and woman is symbolic of our union with Jesus Christ. When we accept the gift of salvation through Jesus' death on the cross, we enter into an agreement or legal contract with Him. It may be a long time before we see Him, but we know we belong to Him. Through the Holy Spirit we begin a new relationship with Christ, and we not only begin to learn more about Him, but He gets to know us—our depth of sincerity and trust, our human weaknesses, the extent of our willingness to do what He wants. As we experience His love, understanding, patience, and gentleness, our love for Him grows stronger and deeper until finally, at the appointed time, He will take us to the home He has prepared for us.

This is what is symbolized in the "marriage of the Lamb" in Revelation 19:7. Again, Jesus Christ is referred to as a Lamb, just as He was when He took the book and opened the seals in Revelation 5. We know that He is the Bridegroom. The Bride will be comprised of those who have placed their faith and trust in God and have accepted His way of salvation. The Bridegroom (Christ) will then take His bride (the believers) to the new home He has prepared—the New Jerusalem.

But we notice something else in verses 7 and 8. The Bride is said to have "made herself ready." How will she go about doing this? Prior to participating in the marriage of the Lamb, "we shall all stand before the judgment seat of Christ" (Romans 14: 10). At that time we will be judged according to all that we have done on earth, whether good or bad. It will be like seeing our whole life passing before our eyes. Every good deed and every bad act will come under the scrutiny of Jesus Christ. Rewards based on our activities in this life will then be handed out.

THE BATTLE

After catching a glimpse of the happiness and joy to be experienced by participants in the marriage of the Lamb, John's attention was diverted back to earth. He saw the armies of the world massing for the most gruesome, bloody, horrendous battle of all time—the Battle of Armageddon.

War is nothing new to us. We have read of the fierce battles of World Wars I and II, the fighting in Korea and Vietnam, and the Arab/Israeli wars. We cannot pick up a newspaper these days without reading of skirmishes, border disputes, or ideological and political conflicts in some part of the world. However, the major military powers have so far been able to hold gingerly on to a tenuous peace—they have not been directly involved. But with the breaking of the second seal this will change, and the major world powers will get into the act.

We have already seen how the Revised Roman Empire will rise to power again. In order for this to happen, some of the twenty-four states presently included inside the territory of the old Roman Empire will have to be conquered by other states. These twenty-four will be reduced to ten, as symbolized by the ten horns on the beast in chapters 12, 13, and 17. This means there will be war involving parts of Europe, Asia, and Africa.

As the Antichrist's power and influence grows, so will his craving for absolute world control. He will begin to put pressure on the leaders of the ten kingdoms to appoint him as their ruler. However, some of these leaders will not be happy with the idea; and the antichrist will resort to war and subdue three of the kingdoms, whereupon the other seven kingdoms will promptly surrender.

Then will come the time when the rest of the nations will realize that they must either defeat the Antichrist or be dominated by him. So they will make plans to attack. This could be the time when 200 million Red Chinese will march across Asia to cross the Euphrates River (Revelation 9:14, 16). But the Antichrist will hear about these plans and in a rage will descend on them with his troops and conquer them. He will then incorporate these former enemies into his own army and will give the orders for them to assemble in the plain of Meggido for the final onslaught on Israel. The unclean spirits of the sixth vial will have done their job in inciting the nations to war, and the stage will be set. Millions of troops will be poised and ready to attack at the signal.

But wait! We see something going on in heaven! According to John, heaven will open and riding out in majesty and power will be a rider on a white horse. Who will this rider be? None other than Jesus Christ—but not the Jesus Christ who walked the dusty roads of Palestine, who graciously and gently ministered to the needs of those around Him, who taught a message of love and forgive-

110

ness, who meekly submitted to the humiliating mockery and attacks of the Roman soldiers. This will be the Christ who is commander in chief of God's heavenly army, who rides out with the authority of the Almighty behind Him, who sets forth to claim the Kingdom of the earth which rightfully belongs to Him. With vengeance and purpose He will lead out the heavenly armies to war against the nations in retaliation for their mistreatment of Israel and for their complete godlessness. God will step in and intervene on behalf of His people, Israel.

This will be the time for Satan and Christ to meet in combat to determine who really is in control and who will rule over the nations of the earth. The nations will think they are there to fight against Israel, but in reality they will have been gathered to fight for Satan against the armies of heaven. Satan will be a deceiver to the end!

Who will make up the heavenly armies that John saw riding on white horses behind their Leader? The redeemed and resurrected believers of all time will be included in these armies, as well as all the angels of heaven. What a sight: millions of people, all dressed in white and riding on white horses! To those assembled for battle on earth this heavenly host will probably look like a huge white cloud.

We can only speculate as to how this battle between the nations of the earth and the armies of heaven will be fought. Perhaps God will unleash some of the supernatural power He used at creation, or perhaps nuclear power will be utilized. Whatever the method, the result will be the same: there will be carnage and devastation such as man has never seen or ever will see again. The combined forces of Satan and Antichrist will be totally defeated. All the earthly armies will be destroyed. The carnage will be devastating and millions of bodies will cover the valley. Vultures, hawks, and all sorts of animals and birds of prey will feast on the flesh of these bodies. Revelation 14:14-20 tells us that for 184 miles this valley will look like a river of blood. It will be so deep that the flow will come up to the horses' bridles. What a horrifying sight!

Now, with the nations destroyed and the Antichrist and the False Prophet defeated, the way will be made clear for Jesus Christ to set up a divine government on earth. This last great calamity, coupled with the defeat of his leaders, will totally squash man's rebellion against God. He will be ready to acknowledge and accept the sovereignty of Christ.

But what will happen to the Antichrist and the False Prophet? Will they die too? No, a special judgment is reserved for them. Revelation 19:20 reveals what will happen to them.

THE DEFEAT

The Antichrist and the False Prophet will be put down, after the armies of the world have been practically wiped out. The rebellious attitude of man will be changed to one of submission. But Satan will still be alive and well. Unless something is done about Satan, it won't be long before he once again will be deceiving men and luring them away from God and into his evil schemes. Revelation 20:1-3 reveals what will happen to Satan.

112

THE FIRST RESURRECTION

Revelation 20:6 begins: "Blessed and holy is he that hath part in the first resurrection." What is the first resurrection? This refers to the resurrection of the righteous and constitutes several separate events.

The first resurrection will have occurred when all those who had died "in Christ"—all the people in the Old Testament and all those in the New Testament who have put their trust in Messiah/Jesus Christ—have been released from their graves and transported into the presence of God. Simultaneously, all those who have accepted Jesus Christ and His way of salvation and who are still alive will be "caught up" in the Rapture and ushered into God's presence. The 144,000 Jews sealed during the Tribulation period will also later be raptured. Finally, a multitude of Tribulation saints who have been beheaded because they would not worship the Beast nor receive his mark on their foreheads will also meet in heaven. These component events will make up the first resurrection.

Earlier we saw that all these people will be represented by the twenty-four elders around the throne of God. Now that the whole drama has unfolded, we know how each group will come to be among the multitude who will gather to worship in the presence of God.

11

THE AGE
OF PEACE

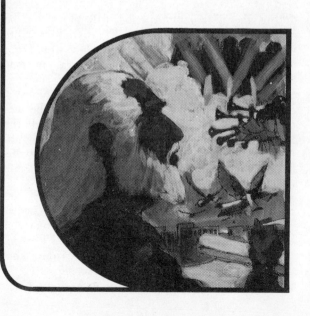

In the fall of 1975 some seven thousand Christians gathered together in a Midwestern city for the sole purpose of praising God. The convention had been advertised as a "Praise Gathering for Believers" and was a combination of worship and singing praises to the Lord. Almost every downtown hotel and motel was filled to capacity. Restaurants had waiting lines a half block long.

Yet not in all that crowd of people was a frown seen or a grumble heard. No one pushed ahead of someone else in line. No one complained about the long wait to be served. Although worship services were held at 8:30 a.m., the early morning breakfast crowds were cheerful and happy. In hotel corridors small groups of people gathered together to discuss the day's activities and even to sing some of the songs and hymns of praise they had learned. Others got acquainted with believers from other sections of the country. Some had come as far as two thousand miles to attend the gathering.

The watchword of those days seemed to be expressed in the words of the oft-heard song, "Getting Used to the Family of God":

> *Going to heaven,*
> *Enjoying the trip,*
> *Getting used to the family*
> *I'll spend eternity with.*
> —Bill Gaither

Can you imagine a scene like this magnified to include the whole world and to last forever? Can you think what it would be like to see smiling, happy faces everywhere and to hear your favorite hymns played over the loudspeakers in grocery and department stores? Why, it would be like having the Christmas spirit all year long!

Well, believe it or not, there will come a day when life here on earth will be just like that. It's called the Millennium.

PEACE

As we pick up John's vision in Revelation 20:4 we hear him say:

> *And I saw thrones, and they sat upon them, and judgment was given unto them: and I saw the souls of them that were beheaded for the witness of Jesus, and for the word of God, and which had not worshipped the beast, neither his image, neither had received his mark upon their foreheads, or in their hands; and they lived and reigned with Christ a thousand years.*

Our attention is drawn to thrones on which the saints will sit. We are first directed to consider those beheaded during the Tribulation period. They will lose their lives for the witness of Jesus and the gospel. They will refuse to take the mark

116

of the beast or to worship his image. Although they are not mentioned here, we know that all the saints raptured at the beginning of the Tribulation period, as well as the 144,000 Jews, will also be present, sitting on thrones. The wicked dead will not be resurrected until after the thousand-year peace reign. There will be no second chance for them.

This period is referred to as the seventh dispensation or the Kingdom. This will be the last dispensation before the curse placed on man in the book of Genesis is removed.

All through the Bible we find references to this Millennial Kingdom. In Ephesians it is called "the dispensation of the fulness of times" (Ephesians 1: 10). The prophets Isaiah and Ezekiel referred to it many times as "that day." (See Isaiah 24:21; Ezekiel 48:35.) Other scriptures call it:

1. "the day of the Lord" (Zechariah 14:1)
2. "the kingdom of heaven" (Matthew 18:3)
3. "the regeneration" (Matthew 19:28)
4. "the consolation of Israel" (Luke 2:25)
5. "the redemption in Jerusalem" (Luke 2:38)
6. "the times of restitution of all things" (Acts 3: 21)
7. "the ages to come" (Ephesians 2:7)
8. "the kingdom of Christ and of God" (Ephesians 5:5)

We have already seen that the Antichrist and the False Prophet will be cast into the lake of fire. Satan will be bound and cast into the bottomless pit. The earth will then enter a thousand-year period of universal peace and prosperity. Here is how it will be:

The government of this time will be a theocratic government. God will be the supreme head, and

Jesus Christ will rule under the Father. The Davidic Covenant, to rule Israel, will be fulfilled in Christ as promised in 2 Samuel 7:8, "Now therefore so shalt thou say unto my servant David, Thus saith the Lord of hosts, I took thee from the sheepcote, from following the sheep, to be ruler over my people, over Israel"; and again in 2 Samuel 7:16, "And thine house and thy kingdom shall be established for ever before thee: thy throne shall be established for ever."

The apostles will each rule one of the twelve tribes of Israel. In Luke 22:29, 30 Christ told them: "And I appoint unto you a kingdom, as my Father hath appointed unto me; That ye may eat and drink at my table in my kingdom, and sit on thrones judging the twelve tribes of Israel." The saints will rule smaller provinces as kings and priests as we saw in Revelation 20:4.

Jerusalem will be rebuilt and will be the world capital—an international city serving as earth's headquarters, with the new Temple being the world capitol building. Each nation will be represented by its most illustrious ambassadors, who will journey to Jerusalem once a year to pay homage to Jesus Christ and acknowledge Him as king.

There will be civil and religious laws, for the government of all nations will be based upon God's Word: "Thou shalt love the Lord thy God. . . . [and] thy neighbour as thyself" (Matthew 22:37-39).

There will be one universal religion. Salvation in all its fullness and divine healing will be available to all. The Holy Spirit will be poured out upon all mankind, and the glory of God will be manifest continually.

Peace and prosperity will prevail universally. Material blessings will fill the earth, and the fruitful seasons will continue without interruption. Even the natures of the animals will be changed as indicated in Isaiah 11:6-9.

Doesn't that sound like heaven on earth? It will be—but not for everyone! The Bible tells us that certain classes of people will not inherit the Kingdom. In 1 Corinthians 6:9, 10 Paul listed eleven sins and said that those who practice them will be excluded: unrighteousness, fornication, idolatry, adultery, effeminacy, theft, covetousness, drunkenness, reviling, and extortion. Galatians 5:19-21 gives us the same list and adds: lasciviousness, sorcery, hatred, strife, jealousy, wrath, factions, seditions, heresies, envyings, and revelings.

REBELLION

While the Millennial period will be one of peace and joy on earth, these will be maintained mostly by the iron rule of Christ. Some will still be rebels at heart, although they will have been forced to submit to an authoritarian government ruled solely by God through Christ. They will be inwardly vexed and enraged at the restrictions placed on them. Others will have become self-righteous while living under ideal conditions and will see no need for salvation. Once again man will think he can "go it alone." These persons will have to be dealt with before God can establish His kingdom.

Thus, at the end of the one thousand years, Satan will be released from his prison and "shall go out to deceive the nations which are in the four

119

quarters of the earth" (Revelation 20:8).

Once and for all God will give man the opportunity to choose between His kingdom and Satan's. The final stage will be set! Satan's big moment will arrive! He will have one more chance to overthrow the rule of Christ and to establish his own kingdom of sin and depravity. Satan will go abroad to the nations and have no difficulty arousing the greed and covetousness of an immense army of sinful men—"the number of whom is as the sand of the sea." (Read Revelation 20:7-9.)

Apparently, God will make short work of this insurrection. The Bible covers it in one sentence: "and fire came down from God out of heaven, and devoured them." In a flashing moment multiple thousands will be consumed by fire from heaven. Satan will have his day. Then he will be defeated once and for all. John sees that he will be "cast into the lake of fire and brimstone" (Revelation 20:10).

JUDGMENT

Do you remember the throne of judgment at the beginning of the Millennial period? Well, we are told there was a rainbow around it. At the end of the Flood, God set the rainbow in the sky as a sign of His covenant of mercy toward His people. (See Genesis 9:13-15.)

But there will be no rainbow around the Great White Throne. The day of reckoning will be at hand—God's mercy will no longer prevail. He will have become a God of justice and retribution.

This will be the moment of truth for all the wicked dead—all the unrepentant sinners. The books will be opened, with the evidence there for all to see. Ungodly men will be brought before the throne to be judged "according to their works."

What does the phrase "according to their works" mean? Consider the following seven points on which the wicked dead will be judged:

1. The account of personal acts (Matthew 12:36)
2. The rule of memory (Luke 16:25)
3. The account of the Word of God (John 12:28)
4. The rule of conscience (Romans 2:12)
5. The rule of Moses (Romans 2:12, 13)
6. The rule of character (Hebrews 3:8-10)
7. The account of the book of life (Revelation 3:5)

Salem Kirban in his *Prophecy New Testament* describes the scene before us: "The lost who have both previously been spiritually dead and physically dead are made alive at the Second Resurrection. They are given resurrection bodies and they are brought into the presence of God for this judgment." (Kirban, *Prophecy New Testament,* 1973, p. 422.)

Sentence will be pronounced—the fate of the wicked will be a terrible one. They will be tormented in the lake of fire for all eternity. Having made an irreversible decision to cling to their evil ways, despite all God's warnings and pleadings, they will experience an eternal separation from God—the second death.

God's work will then be done. What was begun in Genesis will have, indeed, been finished in Revelation.

12

ETERNAL
RECONCILIATION

God's plan and design for man was that he multiply and populate the earth. God wanted to bless and enjoy fellowship with him. So man was given the whole earth as his domain, and all the indescribable beauty of God's creation for his enjoyment and pleasure. (Read Genesis 1:27-30.)

In that creation God made provision for the necessary nourishment to keep this intricate and incredible machine called man healthy and happy. Everything man desired or needed was available to him.

Man could have gone on for ever and ever enjoying what God had provided and planned. But he messed it all up. When Adam and Eve disobeyed God, sin entered the world and the perfection of God's handiwork was marred from then on.

Even though creation became irrevocably tainted by sin, God had a plan to cleanse man from this curse. Jesus Christ was born into the world, and by His death on the cross took our sins and we became reconciled to God.

At this point in our quarterly sojourn, we come to the end of time and the beginning of eternity. But before this can start certain events must take place. Having dealt with man, God must turn His attention to creation. Everything that is tainted or marred by sin must be destroyed before God can come and inhabit the earth with man, His ultimate creation.

There is indeed going to be an end of the world! The Bible often refers to it. But the inference that the earth is going to be completely obliterated is not correct. A more exact interpretation would be a transition or passing from one phase into another. The earth as we know it is not headed for extinction. It will merely go through a process of regeneration to rid it of all sin, in much the same way that man is spiritually regenerated by accepting God's plan of redemption.

Revelation, chapter 21, opens with the words, "And I saw a new heaven and a new earth: for the first heaven and the first earth were passed away; and there was no more sea." That's all John told us about this cataclysmic happening. For a more detailed description of what will take place read 2 Peter 3:10.

If this seems fanciful to you, let's look at some scientific facts. It is well known that the atmosphere is composed of several gaseous elements, nitrogen and oxygen being the two predominating substances. Oxygen is a basic necessity for all combustion. In fact, burning is merely the oxidation of matter. Whether in the slow combustion of metabolism in our bodies, or in the immediate violent combustion of gas in a motor's cylinder or a bomb, oxidation is essential. The air about us is composed largely of this combustible gas. The other element in air is nitrogen, the basic element in high explosives like dynamite and TNT.

Water is also present in the atmosphere, and water consists of oxygen and hydrogen. Hydrogen is the highly explosive gas once used for inflating dirigibles, but, because of its high combustibility, has been replaced. Perhaps you have seen pictures of the disaster of the *Hindenburg* in 1937. Think of the air you breathe as consisting of these various gases. Every one of them is a combustible element if the proper combinations and conditions are present. (Adapted from M. R. De Haan, M.D., *Revelation,* pp. 288, 289.)

We have already seen the dire consequences that will result from God lifting His controlling hand from the earth—earthquakes, pollution, famine, diseases, Satanic attacks on man himself, and all the horrors of the seals, trumpets, and vials judgments. But through all this the balance of the atmosphere will be left undisturbed. Think, however, what could happen if God were to alter that balance. What Peter said about the heavens passing away with a great noise suddenly becomes quite feasible. There would be one tremendous explosion!

This earth on which we live is approximately twenty-five thousand miles in circumference and eight thousand miles in diameter. It is formed like a hollow ball, with an outer crust and an inner core of seething, boiling, molten elements. It is this molten liquid that belches out when a volcano erupts, leaving a blackened, charred wake.

We really are living on a potential "bomb," which could explode at any time but which doesn't because God controls the elements. However, a time will come when God will lift His control and the elements will melt with fervent heat, and the earth and everything on it will be burned up. This will all be part of the purifying process.

In his book *World Aflame* Billy Graham comments, "Whatever is not suited for the new life of the new world will be destroyed. This is what some call the end of the world, but the world will never end. It will only be changed into a better world."

The question arises, "What will happen to all the people on the earth while these changes are taking place?" The Scriptures do not tell us exactly, but perhaps they will be taken up into the New Jerusalem to wait there until the earth is renovated. Whatever happens, we know that they will be "with the Lord" (1 Thessalonians 4:17).

A NEW HEAVEN

The heavens we look at each night are beautiful, but how much more beautiful will they be when they have been retouched, cleansed, and brightened up from all their old disorders and imperfections! All violence will be removed. There will be no more tornadoes to level cities and bring terror to the inhabitants; there will be no more hailstones to wipe out crops; there will be no more hurricanes to wash away houses and lands. The new heavens will be as orderly and perfect as those created in Genesis 1:1-8.

A NEW EARTH

It seems very obvious why nothing more is said about the new earth that John saw. It must have been indescribable! We are awed by the majestic mountains of the earth today, inspired by the stately trees of the forest, fascinated by the intricacy of delicate flowers. But this is still only the old earth in its soiled and working garb, subject to the miseries brought on by a godless world.

Think what its regeneration will bring: No more pollution, no more digging and plowing to grow food, no more thorns and thistles, no snakes lying curled under rocks, no venomous spiders, no wild animals waiting in ambush to attack. What a wonderful place it will be! We will enjoy the perfection of creation without the imperfections sin has introduced.

A NEW JERUSALEM

Next John saw an amazing sight—a city coming down from heaven. We don't know how this will happen; but when we consider all the supernatural events that will take place prior to this, we know it is possible. This city will be the New Jerusalem; and as it descends, John said, it will look "prepared as a bride adorned for her husband" (Revelation 21:2). This is the city where the believers who constitute the bride of Christ will live.

The exact location of this New Jerusalem is not stated. Some believe it will hover just above the earth something similar to the way the pillar of cloud and the pillar of fire did when the Israelites were traveling through the Wilderness. Others say it will actually descend to earth.

As a comparison for the way John must have felt trying to describe this fantastically beautiful city, imagine taking a primitive, blindfolded native from an isolated jungle. Set him down at New York's Kennedy Airport for a while and remove the blindfold. Then transport him back to his jungle and ask him to tell his friends and relatives what he has seen. If he tells them he saw a jumbo jet land with full flaps down, they will stare blankly at him. But if he tells them he saw something like a gigantic flying elephant, they will break into smiles of understanding.

This was John's dilemma. He had to try to describe what he saw based on his own limited knowledge and understanding.

God is a master architect. The New Jerusalem He has planned for His people will be His ultimate design. It will be enormous—a square, measuring 1,500 miles on each side. Commentators see it as a giant cube towering 1,500 miles into the sky, with streets 1,500 miles long! If this city were to be placed over the United States, its base would stretch from Maine to Florida and from the Atlantic Ocean to Colorado!

A NEW TEMPLE

In verse 22 John said, "And I saw no temple therein." Imagine God building a magnificent new city with no need of an imposing temple. Think of the fame and glory some of the temples of our day have brought to their cities: St. Peter's Basilica in Rome, Notre Dame Cathedral in Paris, St. Paul's Cathedral in London, the Mormon Tabernacle in Salt Lake City, and St. Patrick's Cathedral in New York, to name a few.

But this New Jerusalem will have no temple in the traditional sense. Why not? The verse continues: "for the Lord God Almighty and the Lamb are the temple of it." Edifices, symbols, and ceremonials will no longer be necessary. God will hold direct and open communion with His people.

When Jesus walked with His disciples on earth, they had a temple wherever He was. Along the shores of Galilee, in the mountains away from the crowds, surrounded by people in the towns, in a little fishing boat, wherever His divine presence was, there they had a temple. They could talk to Him as a friend; they could share their burdens and problems with Him. They had easy access to His presence. This is what it will be like in the New Jerusalem. The Lord God Almighty and the Lamb (Jesus) will share fellowship with all the redeemed in immediate and direct communication.

A NEW ILLUMINATION

Another thing this city will not need is a lighting system. There will be no need for huge generators to produce electric light power; nor will there be any need for flicking switches or pulling cords, "for the glory of God did lighten it, and the Lamb is the light thereof." Exodus 34:29 tells us how Moses' face shone after he had spent time in God's presence. When Saul of Tarsus was on his way to Damascus to persecute the Christians, a light brighter than the noonday sun shone down on him and blinded him (Acts 26:13). On the Mount of Transfiguration light radiated from the body and clothing of Jesus (Luke 9:29). Mortal eyes cannot stand to look at the brightness of the glory of God, but with immortal eyes we will be able to walk in the light of the Lamb that will surround us forever.

A NEW LIFE-STYLE

It's hard for us to imagine what life will be like in God's eternity. Perhaps the change we can most easily identify with is that there will be no more tears, sorrow, or crying—no more tears over the

129

loss of a parent, relative, or friend, because there will be no more death. There will be no more tears of loneliness, disappointment, or defeat. All the things and people who have caused us hurt and heartache won't matter anymore, for "God shall wipe away all tears from their eyes" (Revelation 21:4).

We can almost picture a loving, heavenly Father gently wiping away the tears of those who have cried in hunger, who have suffered cruelty and torture, who have never known anything but want and need. Those who have endured racking pain will never experience it again, because there will be no pain in heaven. All the things associated with the curse of sin on this world will have passed away, and everything will be made new.

Whatever man needs for his eternal health and life will be provided by God in the New Jerusalem. There will be a "river of water of life" (Revelation 22:1), and on either side of this river there will be trees that will produce twelve different kinds of fruit—a different kind each month.

The nations will live in peace and harmony, and their ambassadors will go in and out of the New Jerusalem as they bring tribute to almighty God. The door to the city will never close, so man will never again be shut out from God's presence.

ETERNITY

How long is eternity? Eternity is forever. Try to imagine that this earth on which we live is nothing but sand. Now try to imagine that a little bird capable of flying through space to a faraway planet takes one grain of sand at a time with him, and

130

that the round trip takes a thousand years. Then try to imagine how long it would take him to move the whole earth, a grain of sand each thousand years. It's more than the finite mind can comprehend. Yet, this still would not be the end of eternity!

In 1 Corinthians 2:9 we read, "Eye hath not seen, nor ear heard, neither have entered into the heart of man, the things which God hath prepared for them that love him." Eternity with God will be more wonderful than we could possibly dream. Reigning and helping God administer the affairs of a beautiful, well-ordered, sinless earth will be an experience to which we can look forward with joy and anticipation.

But, conversely, eternity away from God will defy imagination in its horrors. There will be endless torment and remorse at what might have been. Memory will recall the times we could have turned to God and didn't, the things and people we valued more highly than our relationship with Jesus Christ, and our costly indecision that put off our salvation until it was too late.

And it will all be so final! There will be no possibility of ever getting a second chance.

Eternal reconciliation or eternal separation? The choice is ours—*now*.

SURVEYING
THE SCENE

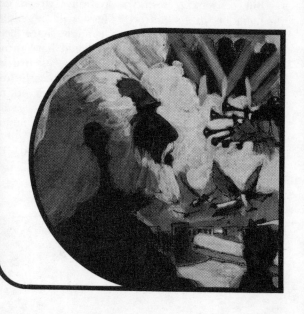

Bible Reading:

Psalm 14:2; Hebrews 9:22
Revelation 1:1, 3, 10, 11
1 Thessalonians 4:16, 17
Revelation 5:1; 7:4; 8:2; 11:3
Zechariah 5:11; Revelation 18:10
13:1, 4, 11, 12; 15:1; 16:1
19:7, 11, 14, 19; 20:4, 11, 12; 21:1, 2; 22:5

One of the two most important events to take place on earth between creation and the present day was the birth of Jesus Christ in Bethlehem. Prior to this, men had lived according to conscience and the Law. With the birth of Jesus God's pattern for living changed. Jesus Christ became the link between God and man, and instead of man placing his faith and trust in a slain lamb, he now could place his faith in a living Person. However, God had decreed that only by shedding of blood could we be made righteous, so Jesus had to suffer and die on the cross as a vicarious sacrifice for all.

Following the resurrection of Jesus Christ the Church Age was instituted. We are still living in the Church Age, which will be consummated at the Rapture. This simply means that after His death and resurrection, He founded the Church, and the early members were those who placed their faith in Him as Lord and personal Savior. Instead of the traditional method of going to the priest for forgiveness of sins, people now could obtain forgiveness through acceptance of Jesus Christ and His teachings.

When Jesus ascended into heaven, He left His disciples and the early church members with an almost impossible task. He said, "Go ye into all the world, and preach the gospel to every creature" (Mark 16:15). How could a band of semiliterate folk preach the gospel of Jesus to the whole world? Especially how could they do it when Jesus Himself wasn't around anymore? Who would give them the guidance they needed? Who would encourage them when the going got rough?

God knew that they and all who followed them down through the ages would need a lot of help if they were to overcome in this world, so He sent His Holy Spirit to be His representative on the earth. The all-encompassing ministry of the Holy Spirit would convict of sin, give men the encouragement they needed, guide them, and minister to their every need. (See John 14:16-26; 16:7-15.)

Centuries have passed, and the ministry of the Holy Spirit is as effective today as it was in the days of the early church. Tragically, though, the spirit of Babylonianism (the cult of godlessness begun by Nimrod) crept into the church; and she got sidetracked from her primary job of winning the lost to Christ. It became much easier for her to be caught up in the liturgy and trappings of a formal church than to commit herself to an unseen Master and obey the leading of the Holy Spirit. The church's attention got diverted, and many things crept in which should never have become a part of the church of Jesus Christ.

John was inspired by God to write about some

of these things in the letters to the seven churches. Although there was a different point of emphasis for each church, we today can take all seven of them and apply them to the church situation of our time and to each of us as individuals:

1. *Remember!* You started out well, but you're slipping now. Your works and efforts are great, but your love means much more.
2. *Fear not!* Don't be afraid of the hard circumstances of your life. Remain faithful, and you will receive your reward.
3. *Be holy!* Don't dabble in questionable practices. Don't compromise your beliefs for fleeting popularity.
4. *Choose!* What is to be the motivating force of your life? Is it self-interest or God's will?
5. *Be real!* The world is full of phonies. Don't hide behind a facade. Don't pretend a spirituality you do not possess.
6. *Stand fast!* Don't be blown about and swayed by the attitudes of the world around you. Place your feet solidly on the Word of God.
7. *Repent!* Don't stay in your lukewarm condition. Take a definite step toward God and His way.

From looking at the past, let's take a look at the present. One of the major indications that God's time clock is rapidly advancing is the status of the nation of Israel. This little nation has always been a bone of contention among the other nations. They seem to be either for her or against her. Even when scattered to the four corners of the earth, the Jews retained their own identity and were never absorbed into the national culture of the countries in which they resided. Now they are once more a nation; and the spirit of courage, independence, sacrifice, and pride that is so much a part of their heritage is now banding them together to make their nation something of which to be proud. They are working together to miraculously transform Israel into a "garden" land—fruitful, productive, and beautiful.

Many things are going to happen in the future as the end of this age approaches. To try and get an overall picture of these coming events, let's imagine that we can stand off in space and watch events as they occur. We'll speed up time, and move right along with them as they take place.

PROPHECIES ARE FULFILLED

The stage is set. Sitting in the middle of Jerusalem is a magnificent *new temple* as prophesied in Daniel 7 and 9. By means of communications media the *whole world has heard the gospel* of Jesus Christ—even the most primitive tribes in the remote corners of the earth. A *worldwide community* has been established. A cashless society has been formed. No longer do people carry around checkbooks. The big computer debits and credits all transactions directly with the individual's bank. If there is not enough money available, it soon lets everyone know! Everything that was prophesied as having to take place before the return of Christ to the earth has been fulfilled. The Christians wait expectantly.

RAPTURE TAKES PLACE

One day the headlines shout, *MILLIONS DISAPPEAR!* The Rapture has taken place, and Jesus Christ has called all those who belong to Him to meet Him in the air—the dead first; then the living.

(There's a story in the printing trade that the *New York Times'* largest size headline letters have never been used. They are being reserved and kept on file for the headlines announcing the rapture of the Church! How interesting to observe that this worldly newspaper admits to the possibility of this event while many churches act as if it will never happen.)

All these millions of Christians have been transported instantly into the presence of God, and there they will remain during the time of terrible distress and suffering that is now beginning.

WORLD UNREST PREVAILS

The formation of a worldwide community has not proved the answer to the world's severe economic problems. The population explosion has caused acute food shortages, and the leaders never seem to be able to achieve a balance between the "have's" and the "have not's." The Israelis and the Arab nations are still provoking each other. Despite summit meetings and endless talks the threat of war among the major powers is still very real. The world is in a mess. What it needs is a real leader— one who will have the respect of all nations, who can take the reins and sort it all out.

TRIBULATION BEGINS

It's about this time that the first seal is broken, and the Antichrist emerges as a world figure. His silver-tongued persuasion gives him influence and power like no man has ever had before him. He starts off in a low-keyed manner; but as his reputation and power builds, so does his ambition. He decides he will not be content until he rules the world.

One of the first things he does is to befriend Israel. With such an influential leader protecting Israel, the attitude of the world changes towards her, resulting in a period of peace and prosperity never before experienced by Israel.

During this period of development in Israel, 144,000 Jewish evangelists are sealed by God to proclaim His gospel. They preach fervently to all who will listen and cause great annoyance to the Antichrist. He seeks to have them killed; but before he can accomplish this, they are raptured into the presence of God and are safe.

Working alongside the Antichrist is another person referred to as the False Prophet. His ministry is to focus attention on the Antichrist and to cause people to revere and worship him. This individual completes the "Unholy Trinity"—Satan, the Antichrist, and the False Prophet. (He will remain as the Antichrist's henchman to the bitter end, and both will finally share the same fate.)

TRIBULATION INTENSIFIES

The Antichrist, however, does not seem to have all the answers. There are still very serious problems with which to cope. The nations start getting edgy, and wars break out (second seal). Famine becomes a major problem (third seal). Millions of people are dying as a result (fourth seal). Somehow all this has to tie in with the disappearance of all those Christians some while back. The Antichrist then begins a campaign to kill all those who profess to be believers in Jesus Christ (fifth seal).

But then the supernatural occurs. The earth experiences the wrath of God as it is poured out in retribution for the martyrdom of His saints (sixth seal). Then there is a silent pause as all of heaven waits for the next phase of judgments (seventh seal).

In spite of the international upheavals caused by the breaking of the seven seals, humanity still does not turn to God. More pressure is placed on them by the seven trumpet judgments. Hail and fire mixed with blood are rained down on the earth, causing a third of all trees and grass to be burned up (first trumpet). While the earth is still trying to recover from this disaster, a giant blazing mass like a mountain crashes into the sea and turns one-third of it to blood. One-third of the fish in the sea and one-third of all ships on the sea are destroyed (second trumpet). Next, a heavenly body hits the earth and poisons one-third of the rivers and streams, making them bitter and undrinkable (third trumpet). Then a strange occurrence takes place. The light from the sun, moon, and stars is diminished by one-third, making the world dull, cold, and gloomy (fourth trumpet).

The earth is really in a mess. However, so far man himself has been left untouched. Now God begins to deal with him. Demon locusts are released from the bottomless pit, and they viciously attack humanity with stings like scorpions. These stings and the attackers are so terrible that men beg to die, but cannot. Only those who are sealed of God are exempt from these attacks (fifth trumpet). Then the news media announces the mobilization of a gigantic army of persons in the form of demon-like horsemen in the East. This is an army energized by Satan, which will march across Asia and leave one-third of the population lying dead in its wake (sixth trumpet).

Meanwhile two men are causing a great stir on earth. They are the two witnesses who rise to prominence and notoriety for their fearless proclamation of the gospel. For three and a half years they denounce the Antichrist and urge the people to turn to God. When finally they are killed by Antichrist, God resurrects them and the whole world watches as they ascend into heaven. After the undaunted ministry of these two men, nobody can say he does not know the way of salvation.

Another interesting occurrence on earth is the rebuilding of the city of Babylon on its ancient site. Not only is it rebuilt, but it becomes the major trade and commercial center of the world. Rulers, merchants, and tradesmen make fortunes from the business channeled through this bustling metropolis. However, this is a completely godless society. The inhabitants worship money, commerce, power, and all that these bring. Because of this God sentences this city to sudden destruction by fire.

By this time the Antichrist's true nature is revealed. He moves from a tactic of peace to one of crushing power. He declares himself a world dictator and moves to eliminate all opposition. He institutes a program where only those who bear his mark may buy or sell anything. He destroys the religious system symbolized by ancient Babylon and forbids worship of anyone or anything, except himself. He wars against nations and conquers them. This man is Satan's puppet, and all his actions are controlled and dictated by Satan himself.

While all this is going on, the judgments of God

are intensifying. The seven trumpet judgments leads right in to the seven vial judgments. Again, men are afflicted. All those who bear the mark of the beast break out in painful and unsightly sores (first vial). The trumpet judgments affected only "thirds"—the vial judgments affect the whole. *All* the rivers and streams, and *all* the seas are turned to blood and become thick, ill-smelling, and disgusting (second and third vials). The sun burns down with such intensity that men are scorched with the heat (fourth vial). Right after that they are plunged into darkness. Something in these catastrophic occurrences causes them extreme pain, and as Revelation 16:10 says, "They gnawed their tongues for pain" (fifth vial).

The sixth vial judgment occurs as a sequence to the sixth trumpet judgment. The Euphrates River dries up in preparation for the colossal army moving across Asia toward Palestine. Unclean spirits have been busy inciting the nations to war, and they are beginning to amass for the final showdown—the Battle of Armageddon.

CHRIST COMES AGAIN

What are all the Christians doing at this time? Where are all those who went in the Rapture? all those who died during the Tribulation? all of the 144,000 Jews? They are participating in the marriage of the Lamb. Also, everyone has to appear before the throne of Jesus Christ to account for his deeds on earth, and rewards are handed out accordingly. All these believers then become members of God's heavenly army, which rides out under the leadership of Jesus Christ to war against the nations of the earth at Armageddon. This return of

Jesus Christ to earth at this time is called the Second Advent or Revelation.

After the horrifying Battle of Armageddon is fought and the heavenly army is triumphant, Satan is bound and thrown into a pit. The Antichrist and the False Prophet are put down; the nations are subdued; and the way is now clear for Jesus Christ to set up His kingdom on earth.

WORLD IS AT PEACE

This is the introduction of the Millennium—a thousand years of peace. The government that is set up at this time is a theocratic one, with God the supreme head and Jesus Christ ruling under the Father. David rules Israel; the apostles rule the twelve tribes of Israel; the saints rule smaller provinces as kings and priests. Peace and prosperity prevail universally.

However, at the end of the thousand years Satan is released from the pit, and immediately he goes about inciting rebellion. Not everyone living under God's reign has accepted the Kingdom, so Satan easily gathers many followers into his army. God makes short work of this insurrection, however, and they are totally destroyed. Satan is then cast into the lake of fire and brimstone.

WORLD IS JUDGED

This is now the time for the second resurrection, when all the wicked dead are brought before the Great White Throne to be judged by God. They are judged on the basis of conscience, memory, the law of Moses, character, personal acts, the book of life, and the Word of God. Their sentence is a terrible one—banishment to the lake of fire for all eternity. Their decision to cling to their evil ways despite all God's warnings and pleadings carries dreadful consequences.

NEW AGE IS INTRODUCED

After a period of violent upheaval and renovation, God restores the earth and the heaven to their state of perfection before sin entered the world. The New Jerusalem descends from heaven and a new age is introduced—an age without pain, suffering, cruelty, torture, hunger, disease, war, strife, and struggle. God will live with man, and the Lamb will fellowship with His people. "And they shall reign for ever and ever" (Revelation 22:5).

THE CHOICE IS OURS

As we've watched—interested and yet detached —isn't it wonderful to know that all this is actually still in the future. We do not have to be among those who endure the terrible judgments of God; we do not have to make the decision whether we will worship the Antichrist or not; we do not have to forfeit our lives in some horrible death as penalty for declaring our faith. All it takes now is a simple prayer, asking God for forgiveness of our sins and accepting Jesus Christ as Lord of our lives. His Holy Spirit takes control and teaches us how to live according to the way God wants us to live so that one day we may be among those who are caught up in the clouds to meet Jesus, who worship around God's throne, who participate in the marriage of the Lamb, who reign with Him in the Millennium, and who finally spend eternity with God. What a different story it will be for those who reject God's plan of salvation!

BIBLIOGRAPHY

Buxton, Clyne W. *Expect These Things*. Old Tappan, New Jersey: Fleming H. Revell Co., 1973.

Cox, Clyde C. *Apocalyptic Commentary*. Cleveland, Tennessee: Pathway Press, 1959.

De Haan, M.D., and M. R. De Haan. *Revelation*. Grand Rapids, Michigan: Zondervan Publishing House, third edition.

Hull, William L. *Israel: Key to Prophecy*. Grand Rapids, Michigan: Zondervan Publishing House, 1957.

Kirban, Salem. *Prophecy New Testament*. Huntingdon Valley: Salem Kirban, Inc., 1973.

Lindsey, Hal. *There's a New World Coming*. Santa Ana, California: Vision House Publishers, 1973.

Livneh, Micha, and Ze'ev Meshel. *Masada*. Tel Aviv, Israel: National Parks Authority.

Seiss, J. A. *The Apocalypse*. Grand Rapids, Michigan: Zondervan Publishing House.

Van Gorder, John J. *ABC's of the Revelation*. Grand Rapids, Michigan: Zondervan Publishing House, 1952.

Walvoord, John F. *Israel in Prophecy*. Grand Rapids, Michigan: Zondervan Publishing House, 1962.